# Catch Them Thinking and Writing

## David Whitehead

SkyLight

Training and Publishing Inc.

**Catch Them Thinking and Writing**

Published by SkyLight Training and Publishing Inc.
2626 S. Clearbrook Drive, Arlington Heights, IL 60005
800-348-4474, 847-290-6600
Fax 847-290-6609
info@iriskylight.com
http://www.iriskylight.com

Senior Vice President, Product Development: Robin Fogarty
Manager, Product Development: Ela Aktay
Acquisitions Editor: Jean Ward
Editors: Dara Lee Howard, Sue Schumer
Book Designer: Bruce Leckie
Cover and Illustration Designer: David Stockman
Proofreader: Heidi Ray
Indexer: Schroeder Indexing
Production Supervisor: Bob Crump

LCCCN: 98-60767
ISBN: 1-57517-080-9

2167-6-98McN
Item Number 1596
07 06 05 04 03 02 01 00 99 98    15 14 13 12 11 10 9 8 7 6 5 4 3 2 1

# Dedication

To Cherie, Kate, and Lucy

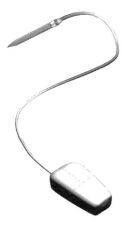

# Contents

**Part I**

## Catch Them Thinking and Writing **Narratives**

**Part II**

# Catch Them Thinking and Writing **Procedures**

**Part III**

# Catch Them Thinking and Writing **Descriptions**

**Part IV**

# Catch Them Thinking and Writing **Reports**

**Part V**

# Catch Them Thinking and Writing **Explanations**

**Part VI**

# Catch Them Thinking and Writing **Arguments and Discussions**

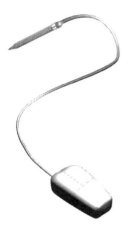

# Foreword

In 1970 Alvin Toffler came out with his shocking pink paperback edition of *Future Shock.* In this seminal work, among his prognostications of a future world, Toffler delineated three skills that students would need in order to flourish in that future society. He discussed the skill of relating to others, the skill of learning how to learn, and the skill of making good choices.

In *Future Shock* Toffler alluded to a diverse, multicultural society reflected in the shrinking global community and predicted a need to relate to others. He alluded to a society in which lifelong learning—from "womb to tomb"—would be the norm, and applauded the concept of learning *how* to learn. Finally, Toffler alluded to a society of option overload, in which the common man/woman would be bombarded with choices, and highlighted the need for sound decision making and critical thinking.

Now, twenty-eight years later, we see his predictions manifested in our world. And we understand his vision. We proclaim the very same needs to our students: Relate to and care about others; reflect on your learning and learn *how* to learn; and think critically and creatively about your world.

To help our youngsters become accomplished in these skills, David Whitehead provides a teacher resource about conversing, collaborating, and critiquing. In this handy reference called *Catch Them Thinking and Writing,* Whitehead targets classroom teachers in their need for a robust resource on factual writing. In this book, Whitehead provides insight through collaborative exercises in six distinct forms of communication: narratives, procedures, descriptions, reports, explanations, and arguments or discussions.

These six forms of communication, as presented in this quality piece, fully prepare youngsters in those very skills Toffler forecasted: relating to others, learning how to learn, and making sound choices. More specifically, youngsters learn about thinking and writing together in collaborative models that build trusting relationships. They learn how to learn through the six models for communicating ideas and they learn about making good choices through the critical as well as creative thinking required in expository writing.

*Catch Them Thinking and Writing* is a valuable reference for anyone who believes that key life skills involve communicating skillfully and thoughtfully with others, not for a test, but for a lifetime.

—Robin Fogarty
Chicago, May 1998

SkyLight Training and Publishing Inc.

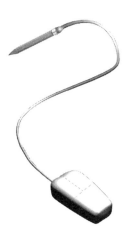

# Acknowledgments

*When the mind is thinking,*
*it is talking to itself.*

—Plato

Learning tends to be more evolutionary than revolutionary, except in the case of writing. When I began teaching writing some years ago, the focus was *how to write*. Today, it is *how to think through writing* and *write through thinking*. The adoption of these beliefs has been nothing short of revolutionary.

Writing this book has affirmed my belief in the power of language as a vehicle for different ways of thinking. It has also strengthened my belief that students need to be taught how to think.

I would like to thank the following people who have contributed their ideas, insights, and support throughout the evolution of this book:

Harry Hood from Dunedin College of Advanced Education for demonstrating what the best teachers of writing can achieve.

Dara Lee Howard, Sue Schumer, Robin Fogarty, Ela Aktay, and the rest of the team at SkyLight for their long-distance support, professionalism, and creativity.

My friends, coworkers, and professional colleagues at the University of Waikato.

Mark Sadoski of Texas A&M University for teaching me (in spite of of Plato) that thinking is not exclusively verbal.

The students and teachers of New Zealand who participated in refining the approaches and frames described in this book.

David Whitehead
May 1998

# Introduction

## What Is This Book About?

This is a book about how to help students think and write factual texts. Although *factual texts* is not a very user-friendly term, it simply means any text intended to convey factual information or to argue a point with objective evidence. Put bluntly, the book aims to demonstrate how we can teach students to think in ways that will allow them to compose different kinds of factual texts—oral and written.

There is considerable interest in the idea of helping students talk and write for a particular purpose, for an identified audience, and by using an appropriate text type. What constitutes appropriateness is often unspecified in our curriculum statements. However, it has been argued by Martin (1985) and Rothery (1986) that students' implicit knowledge of text types is extensive and that one of the teacher's roles is to make this implicit knowledge explicit.

Associated with each factual text type is a factual way of thinking. Some factual thinking is tricky, unnatural, and more taught than caught. For example, students are unlikely to spontaneously use Socratic Questions (see chapter 16) prior to writing an argument; they will need some explicit demonstrations.

Knowledge of how to think and knowledge about the characteristics of factual texts are brought together in this book. For example, if I want students to compose a narrative that outlines what they did during their summer vacation, I might first teach them how to recall and organize their ideas using a timeline/excitement frame (see chapter 1). The timeline/excitement frame encourages the kind of thinking vital to the composition of narratives. I might then demonstrate what written narrative texts look and sound like and provide them with a writing frame within which they can compose a draft of their narrative. In summary, the timeline/excitement frame helps students think, the narrative text demonstrations show them various writing conventions that determine how narratives might be written, and the narrative writing frame provides a structure for writing.

Clearly, a relationship exists between the purpose of a particular factual text and its structure. For example, the purpose of a procedure text is to tell someone how to do something, as in recipes, instruction leaflets, and so on. This purpose gives rise to particular text structures. Procedures have to make clear what materials might be needed to achieve a particular aim and the steps needed to reach a successful conclusion. A procedure is less likely to achieve its purpose if the instructions are given first, the list of materials needed is toward the end, and, finally, you are told what it is you are making.

Society is the genesis of the six factual texts modeled in this book. These texts are social constructions in the sense that society determines the language, structure, and purposes of these texts. Some of these texts are more common than others and some are more powerful in society than others. Consequently, teachers need to obtain authentic models of these six factual text types and demonstrate their form to novice writers.

# How Is the Book Organized?

This introduction is followed by six parts, each treating one text type or genre as follows:

- Narratives—diaries, newspaper articles, histories, or autobiographies
- Procedures—how to fix a leaky faucet, or how to run a nuclear reactor
- Descriptions—specific descriptions, for example, of a pet cat
- Reports—general descriptions, for example, of cats, birds, or cars
- Explanations—why we see lightning before we hear thunder, or how volcanoes erupt
- Arguments—a one-sided view of a topic—and discussions—a two-sided view of a topic

Each part is divided into three chapters. The first chapter in each part describes and models a specific type of factual text. These models may be copied for demonstration purposes. This chapter contains writing frames that illustrate the structure of a factual text and are intended to guide writers and to model thinking frames for demonstration. Thinking frames are designed to help students record and manipulate information prior to writing a specific type of factual text. The frames are designed to evoke specific kinds of factual thinking. These

SkyLight Training and Publishing Inc.

frames are blacklines so they may be photocopied for classroom purposes. Also included in the first chapter of each part are assessment rubrics for each type of factual text and thinking frame.

The second chapter of each part provides oral, visual, and written language activities designed to support the practice of specific techniques useful for the writing of a specific type of factual text. These can be referenced when teachers design their factual thinking and writing programs.

The third chapter of each part provides model programs presented as activities that demonstrate how the thinking and writing frames might be used in practice. Each set of these activities has a similar structure, but within this structure, the activities model numerous approaches to teaching and learning. The overall structure of these lessons is described in detailed at the end of this introduction.

# What Are Factual Frames?

There are two types of factual frames in this book: thinking frames and writing frames.

## Factual Thinking Frames

Factual thinking frames are designed to help students think skillfully prior to composing specific types of factual text. Each thinking frame is linked to a writing frame. For example, the brainstorm thinking frame is designed to help students record and manipulate information prior to using report writing frames, whereas the perspective thinking frame is designed to help students think about two or more sides of an issue prior to using discussion writing frames.

## Factual Writing Frames

Like factual thinking frames, writing frames consist of skeleton outlines that provide scaffolds for students' writing. The frames include different key words or phrases according to the particular text type. They give students an initial structure within which they can concentrate on communicating their message while providing scaffolds to use with a particular text type. Cairney (1990) described frames as a form of probed text recall, and Cudd and Roberts (1989) noted that frames provide a bridge that eases the transition from fiction to factual writing

In summary, each factual writing frame reflects the linguistic characteristics, or generally accepted structures, of a specific type of factual text and is designed to prompt and scaffold student writing. For example, the report writing frames are designed to assist students to write in the present tense about a generic (a general) class of things.

## Some Conventions of Factual Texts

| | Narrative | Procedure | Description | Report | Explanation | Argument/ Discussion |
|---|---|---|---|---|---|---|
| **Tense** | Past | Present | Present | Present | Present | Present |
| **Focus** | Action/ Event | Action/ Event | Object/ Event | Object/ Event | Process | Reflection |
| **Subject** | Specific subject, time, and place | Generic subject, time, and place | Specific subject, time, and place | Generic subject, time, and place | Generic subject, time, and place | Generic subject, time, and place |

*Figure Intro. 1*

Some of the conventions associated with each of the six factual texts are outlined in figure Intro.1. This figure indicates that tense is one indicator of different texts—although only narratives tend to be in the past tense, whereas other texts generally use the present tense.

Subject focus also helps define each text type. Narratives allow us to handle action whereas arguments allow us to be more reflective. Similarly, descriptions allow us to talk about specific things, such as my cat Carla. The subject of a report is more general. Some texts, like narratives, are better at handling concrete things that we can see and do. Other texts, like arguments, allow us to handle abstract ideas.

The links among different types of factual texts, thinking frames, and associated thinking skills are outlined in figure Intro. 2. Each text type is linked to a cluster of critical and creative thinking skills (Fogarty and Bellanca 1986), reinforcing the proposal that when students acquire a new way of factual writing they acquire new ways of thinking. The thinking and writing frameworks are *not intended to be prescriptive*. But students need a working knowledge of factual texts, thinking frames, and associated thinking skills if they are to confidently compose mixed texts that reflect the creative manipulation of information for particular purposes. Indeed, it is important that teachers and students understand that the writing frames are designed *to support draft writing* and that words may be crossed out or substituted, extra sentences may be added, or surplus starters may be crossed out. The frames should be treated as flexible aids, not rigid forms.

# Factual Thinking Frames and Thinking Skills

## THINKING FRAMES

| Narrative | Procedure | Description | Report | Explanation | Argument | Discussion |
|---|---|---|---|---|---|---|
| 1. Critical Thinking<br>2. Timeline/ Excitement | 1. Flow Chart | 1. Character/ Event Set<br>2. Three-Story<br>3. FIND | 1. Meaning<br>2. Brainstorm<br>3. Graphic<br>4. Meaning Web | 1. Event Network<br>2. Explanatory Sketch Board<br>3. Analogy | 1. Discussion Web<br>2. Creative Problem- Solving | 1. Perspective<br>2. Socratic Questions |

## THINKING SKILLS

Perception ⟵————————————————————————⟶ Conception

### Critical and Creative Thinking Skill Clusters

| Sequencing | Sequencing | Attributing Brainstorming | Attributing Brainstorming | Inferencing Sequencing | Analyzing Evaluating | Analyzing Evaluating |
|---|---|---|---|---|---|---|

### Associated Thinking Skills

| Recalling, Composing bias, Questioning, Evaluating, Identifying patterns over time, Identifying cause-and-effect, Inferencing, Generalizing, Linking | | Classifying, Grouping, Questioning, Visualizing, Personifying, Substantiating, Justifying, Elaborating, Comparing and contrasting, Sequencing, Linking, Composing analogies, Clarifying, Observing | | Composing cause and effect, Drawing conclusions, Imaging, Predicting, Generalizing | Composing bias, Composing assumptions, Predicting, Drawing conclusions, Composing analogies, Making decisions, Solving problems, Combining ideas, Considering multiple perspectives | |

*Figure Intro. 2*     Adapted with permission from *Teach Them Thinking: Mental Menus for 24 Thinking Skills,* R. Fogarty and J. Bellanca, 1986.

Further conventions of the six factual texts are outlined in figure Intro. 3. This figure notes that, although these texts are supposed to be objective, there is a subjective dimension in them all—authors can never completely remove themselves from the topic. It also notes that specific types of factual texts are typical of different subjects across the curriculum.

Indeed, each factual text and associated thinking frame is often linked with particular curriculum subjects. These subjects are sometimes called disciplines, which is appropriate since each subject is associated with a particular disciplined way of thinking. In this sense, different types of text are linked to different ways of thinking—and not others. You cannot compose quite the same meaning in a love letter as you can in a scientific report—although it might be fun trying. The conventions of a love letter prevent the inclusion of certain scientific beliefs—they enable the writer to enclose some beliefs and leave out others.

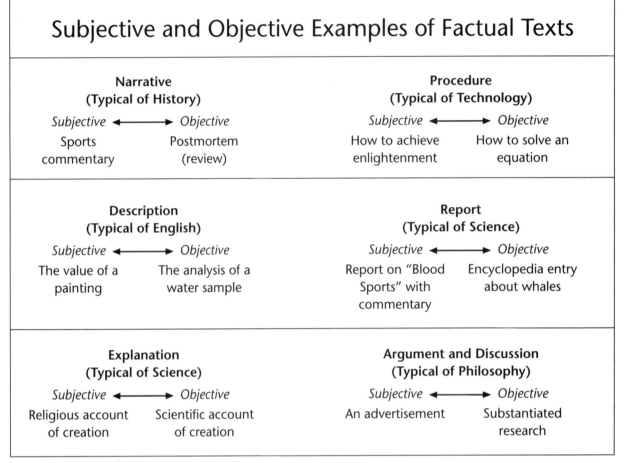

## Subjective and Objective Examples of Factual Texts

**Narrative**
**(Typical of History)**

*Subjective* ←——→ *Objective*

Sports
commentary

Postmortem
(review)

**Procedure**
**(Typical of Technology)**

*Subjective* ←——→ *Objective*

How to achieve
enlightenment

How to solve an
equation

**Description**
**(Typical of English)**

*Subjective* ←——→ *Objective*

The value of a
painting

The analysis of a
water sample

**Report**
**(Typical of Science)**

*Subjective* ←——→ *Objective*

Report on "Blood
Sports" with
commentary

Encyclopedia entry
about whales

**Explanation**
**(Typical of Science)**

*Subjective* ←——→ *Objective*

Religious account
of creation

Scientific account
of creation

**Argument and Discussion**
**(Typical of Philosophy)**

*Subjective* ←——→ *Objective*

An advertisement

Substantiated
research

*Figure Intro. 3*

## Using Factual Frames

Thinking and writing frames are not designed to be straitjackets for
either creativity or literacy, but rather are designed as supportive aids to
prewriting and draft writing. When students understand the various
ways of thinking and the general conventions of various factual texts,
teachers may dispense with the frames.

Consistent with a belief that students should gradually accept
responsibility for learning, teachers might choose to first model the
frames with the whole class. Then, students might benefit from practice
in groups before accepting the challenge of using the frames independently. Most factual frames require gradual introduction. For example,
introducing the brainstorm frame will probably require five or more
activities. Likewise, argument frames become progressively complex and
need to be introduced over several work sessions.

Figure Intro. 2 illustrates that text types are progressively more
abstract and concept-focused, and, consequently, more challenging to
compose. These characteristics may suggest a developmentally based
factual thinking and writing program that begins with a focus on

narratives and moves toward a focus on arguments and discussions. Indeed, Reppens (1994) suggested the progressive introduction of less familiar, more abstract text types, beginning with narratives, then comparing this text type with description, then with more abstract and formal text types. Teachers do not need reminding that even young children can argue!

## Why Use the Frames?

The idea of using text frames is not new (McCarthy and Carter 1994; Hewings and McCarthy 1988). Text frames have been used to present text structure in diagrammatic form with empty labeled boxes representing the various text parts. Writing and thinking frames are designed to help students develop their knowledge of language, of thinking strategies, and of the writing process.

Underpinning the use of frames is a belief that students may never acquire sufficient knowledge of language or of complex thinking strategies without explicit modeling. Not everything is "caught" as in the acquisition of oral language; some things must be taught. Such modeling is consistent with good teaching and learning, whether you hold to a whole language (balanced literacy) or direct instruction approach, as long as this knowledge is taught in meaningful, purposeful, learner-centered contexts, and after students have built up a knowledge of a topic they want to talk or write about.

Indeed, the use of frames has been tried (Wray and Lewis 1995) and found to help students of all ages and abilities. Their wide applicability among students from ages five to sixteen is one of their most positive features. They are particularly useful with students who have average ability, who find factual writing difficult, or who have special needs in literacy. Teachers have noted improved quality and quantity of writing when using frames with these students. In short, the frames are designed to meet the needs of specific students as and when they need them. They are not intended as class worksheets, for within any class there will be students who do not need them.

Teachers should use the frames as temporary scaffolds (Bruner 1986). Like the scaffolding around a building under construction, these frames are gradually removed as students independently cope with the processes of thinking and writing.

# The Structure of Focus Activities

The third chapter of each part provides a series of focus activities that are based on a two-process model of writing (see fig. Intro. 4). The two processes are writing together and writing independently.

# The Two-Process Model of Writing

## Process One: Writing Together

### Before Writing
- Preparation (by the teacher)
- Building knowledge of the topic
- Modeling a thinking frame
- Modeling factual texts
- Modeling a writing frame

### Writing
- Joint construction by
  - Applying a thinking frame
  - Applying a writing frame
- Identifying audience and purpose
- Drafting, revising, and conferencing

## Process Two: Writing Independently

### Before Writing
- Identifying audience and purpose

### Writing
- Translating knowledge into written text
- Revising and conferencing

### After Writing
- Sharing and responding to readers
- Assessing and evaluating

*Figure Intro. 4*

SkyLight Training and Publishing Inc.

Writing together includes modeling and joint construction of a text. Writing independently involves students composing on their own and applying the knowledge and skills acquired while working with the class.

The two-process model is similar to the curriculum cycle or wheel model described by Callaghan, Knapp, and Nobel (1993). During the writing together process, teachers model annotated examples of text type and associated thinking, and they encourage students to identify the text's purpose and notable linguistic features, such as tense. The writing together process also involves teachers and students collaboratively writing, that is, scaffolding. The teacher guides students through the planning and structuring of a joint text, which is written together with the teacher acting as scribe to record students' suggestions on the board or overhead projector.

During the writing independently process, students pursue their interest in the curriculum topic and compose their own text in consultation with other students and the teacher. Students continue to build their knowledge of the topic and teachers continue to model as necessary. The writing independently process ends with sharing and some attempt to critically assess the use of frames, the final products, and the writers' attitudes.

The two-process model of writing combines process and cognitive approaches (Graves 1983; Flower and Hayes 1984) with a genre approach (Rothery 1986).

Aspects of the process and cognitive approaches are reflected in focus activities, which include opportunities for students to generate texts (i.e., build knowledge of a topic and record and manipulate information). Associated with text generation are questioning and inquiry types of thinking. The focus activities also provide students with opportunities to compose texts (i.e., draft and focus their writing). Associated with text composition are elaborating on and evaluating types of thinking. Further, the process and cognitive approaches provide opportunities to revise, conference, edit, publish, and respond. The use of thinking frames to facilitate prewriting is also consistent with these approaches.

The genre approach is reflected in the use of explicit instruction in through thinking and writing frames, the modeling of specific factual text types, and the joint construction of texts.

In relation to this approach, note the strategies outlined in figure Intro. 4.

1. The modeling of thinking and writing frames prior to independent writing

2. Recognition of the writing process (and of its recursive nature)

3. The need for response and reflection as part of any writing program

4. Thorough planning between factual thinking and writing programs, and linking with programs in other curriculum areas

Several beliefs about writing are shared by the process and cognitive and genre approaches. One belief underpinning these three complementary approaches is that students often require a considerable period of conscious thinking about their topic before these thoughts can be translated into words. Subconscious rehearsal often precedes writing. Rehearsal may be assisted further by students' talking, drawing, and reading about their topic prior to writing.

A second belief is that writers can begin the writing process anywhere—with ideas, images, emotions, and words. Although elements in the two-process model (see fig. Intro. 4) are listed in a particular order, writing and thinking processes are recursive. The focus activities should not determine when and where students begin to think and write.

A third belief shared by the approaches is that sometimes students experience writer's block (Bereiter and Scardamalia 1982). One type of block is associated with the task of producing continuous text, that is, text without the turn-taking typical of oral conversation. Focus activities on writing address this potential block by suggesting that teachers and students jointly compose texts.

A second writer's block is associated with the problem of retrieving information from memory. The focus activities again address this by emphasizing the kinds of thinking that might be encouraged before writing, and by helping students build up their knowledge of the topic throughout the activity. Specifically, thinking frames are incorporated into the activities that assist students to record and manipulate what they know and to help them construct new meanings.

A third writer's block is associated with the problem of planning beyond the present sentence. This problem is tackled through the use of writing frames that provide linguistic scaffolds. These frames assist students to move from local to whole-level planning.

A final block is associated with the problem of revision. The focus activities address this in two ways: by using the writing frames for draft writing only, and by jointly constructing and reconstructing drafts.

Further beliefs that underpin these approaches are that students should

- build up their knowledge of the topic,

- decide on genuine purposes for writing,

- decide on the likely audience,

- decide how that audience might influence the way they write,

- become independent by first writing together, then later, writing independently,

- recognize the range of behaviors associated with writing.

(Please note: The detail in the focus activities included in the third chapter of each part is for demonstration purposes only. Teachers are encouraged to choose some of the activities, not all, from each of the two-process phases to help students think and write their factual texts. Teachers are reminded that the primary goal of any thinking and writing program should remain enjoyment and meaning.)

# Long-Term Planning

Figure Intro. 5 provides a broad view of planning. This view suggests components that might be included in a yearlong factual thinking and writing program. The time devoted to each component will vary according to the students' needs. The figure also includes example activities that show how the components might be articulated in practice. (All of the examples are from the procedures text type.)

For example, the recreational and modeling key planning components might be particularly important in programs designed to alter attitudes and acquaint students with how to think factually and with the sounds of factual language. Assessment is crucial at the beginning of any program as it suggests where students are and where teachers might like to take them. The application component features assessment as part of planning in other curriculum areas, and the sharing component gives purpose and authenticity to the program.

Between this broad component level of programming and the detail provided in the focus activities is a middle curriculum level of planning. This planning accompanies the development of any unit, theme, or center of interest. For example, if the class is to focus on conservation for a week or more, the teacher might consider the factual thinking and writing demands of that study. If students are to write a report as part of this focus, then teachers might plan to use the brainstorm frame and a report writing frame.

# Assessment

Student self-evaluations are a crucial component of an overall assessment program. Figure Intro. 6 provides self-assessment starters that might assist students to reflect on their writing progress.

A more complex self-assessment that focuses on the use of thinking frames is provided in figure Intro. 7. The questions included in this figure might guide teachers during a conference with individual students or the whole class, and later, with able high school students, provide a self-assessment guide.

# Key Planning Components

| Planning Component | Description | Examples |
| --- | --- | --- |
| Recreation | Informal composing of factual texts | • Sharing how you repaired something at home prior to a formal show-and-tell session<br>• Telling the class your steps to making the school a more beautiful place<br>• Reading procedures, such as recipes, during free reading or sustained silent reading time.<br>• Writing a procedure to a pen pal |
| Modeling | Demonstrations of how to think and write factual texts | • Collecting a range of different procedures and describing their features<br>• Reading procedures to and with the class and talking about the author's meanings<br>• Demonstrating the use of procedure thinking frames, including the use of flow charts |
| Instruction | Teaching, in a formal sense, how to think and write factual texts | • Using instructional approaches, such as guided reading, with procedure texts<br>• Using signal words as part of a word study or cloze exercise<br>• Using the two-process approach to factual thinking and writing programs |
| Application | Using what you know about thinking and writing factual texts across subjects | • Trying procedures that students have written in another class or with their parents<br>• Taking notes of a procedure demonstrated in a book or on video, using a flow chart |
| Sharing | Telling others what you know about thinking and writing factual texts, and sharing factual texts you have written | • Compiling class folders of procedures<br>• Responding to writers' published procedures<br>• Using flow charts as presentation aids |
| Evaluation | Reflecting on how you wrote a factual text, the meanings you made, the characteristics of the writing, and audience response | • Using procedure thinking and writing assessments<br>• Writing anecdotal records based on conferences<br>• Assisting students to compile a portfolio of procedures<br>• Asking students to keep diaries or dialog journals that describe what they are learning about thinking and writing procedures |

*Figure Intro. 5*

This book will have achieved its purpose when teachers no longer need to use it with their class. That is, of course, the ultimate intent when designing programs—to lead students toward independence as thinkers and writers.

---

## Helping Students Assess Their Factual Writing Skills

Things that I can do before writing a . . .

Things that I know about . . .

Things I can do while writing a . . .

How well I achieved my purpose for writing a . . .

Things that I'm learning how to do . . .

---

*Figure Intro. 6*

# Helping Students Assess Their Use of Thinking Frames

## Purpose

Why did I use this thinking frame? Did it help me write?

## Solution

What (content) did I figure out by using the thinking frame?

## Assumption

What did I assume by using this thinking frame? (For example, I assumed there was more than one solution to a problem when I chose to use a discussion web.)

## Perspective

Did this thinking frame make me think in a particular way? Are there other ways I could have thought about this content? (For example, a timeline/excitement frame might help me think in a time-locked, linear way. However, are there other ways I could think about an event before writing a narrative?)

## Information

What information did the thinking frame allow me to include in my writing? What did the frame prevent me from including? (For example, a timeline/excitement frame might help me to include events in my writing but doesn't prompt me to think critically about those events.)

## Content

Did the thinking frame help me record and think about content clearly?

## Conclusion

Did I base my writing on information contained in my thinking frame? Did this make sense?

## Implication

Am I going to use the thinking frame again to help me write?

*Figure Intro. 7*

SkyLight Training and Publishing Inc.

# Catch Them
Thinking and Writing
Narratives

# Overview of Thinking and Writing Narratives

**Narratives are**

Time-sequenced

In the past tense

Event-ordered

**Writing narratives means using**

Narrative Writing Frames

News Story Frame

**Thinking Narratives means using**

Critical Thinking Frames

Timeline/Excitement Frames

**Narrative thinking involves**

Sequencing

Recalling

Composing bias

Questioning

Evaluating

Identifying patterns over time

Identifying cause-and-effect

Inferencing

Generalizing

Linking

**Types of narratives include**

Personal

Imaginative

Factual

*Figure Part 1.1*

SkyLight Training and Publishing Inc.

# WHAT IS a Narrative?

CHAPTER 1

The quick answer to the question of what is a narrative is that it is the kind of talking and writing we do most often.

- When we talk about what happened during the day, we are composing an oral narrative.

- When we write in a diary, we are composing a written personal narrative likely to contain comment. But that's okay because narratives are seldom neutral, unless you're tape-recording an autopsy.

Narratives use factual information about an object, character, or event to convey narrative information. They may reconstruct a past event, whether the event is imaginative or within the author's experience. Narratives are time-sequenced and include personal reflections or comment. Some narratives use a setting, initiating the structure of an event, complication, or resolution; others simply employ a structure consisting of a listing of events.

So, there are different types of narratives, and there are no pure narratives apart from those found in linguists' heads. Narratives are even found inside other types of writing. For example, when someone is arguing a point of view, that individual may tell about an incident that supports his or her position. Sometimes, sports announcers seem to be commenting more than narrating!

Although narratives serve a range of purposes, they are still easy to spot. Here are their characteristics:

- Most often, they are about something that happened in the past.

- Most are written in the third person. However, personal narratives in a diary may use the first person, especially when the writer reflects on events.

The events described in a narrative are usually ordered in a time sequence. This order is explicitly signaled with such words or phrases as

| first | before | next | eventually |
| last | after | then | on the second day |
| later | during | finally | |

Believe it or not, these words are alternatives to the oft-used "And then . . . , and then . . ." that young writers are so fond of using.

Sometimes it is hard to find the border between the narrative continuum and other kinds of factual writing. *Star Trek* is an imaginative science fiction narrative, that is, it is science fiction but episodes include factual information, and it is an event-sequenced form of narrative. But, at the other end of the continuum is the ship's log or postmortem log. These are, strictly speaking, informational narratives of a factual type.

# Why Think and Write Narratives?

Grade 1 teachers know that first writing is often narrative writing— what happened at home or what happened over the weekend. Students of this age like writing about real, recent, and concrete experiences that involved them. They tend to talk and write narratives before other nonfiction texts, such as discussion (see chapter 16), perhaps because narratives lend themselves to telling about concrete events whereas discussions lend themselves to thinking about abstract ideas. Of course, young students do discuss and do argue or persuade—ask any parent or teacher. And they should never be dissuaded from attempting any type of writing.

Links between cognitive development and narrative writing (Vygotsky 1978; Applebee 1978) suggest we might expect different types of thinking represented in different narrative structures. For example, Grade 1 students' narratives may be random collections of statements or events. Later, these may take on a sense of unity, cohesion, and sequence that enables writers to develop a theme or moral. On another level, the narratives of Grade 1 students tend to be self-centered, whereas older students compose more decentered texts that enable them to argue points of view.

However, teachers need to be critical about accepting a sequence of cognitive development or a sequence in the development of language forms. There is no fixed sequence. Students are capable of composing a range of narratives at any age, just as Grade 1 students are capable of formal operational thinking when narrating about real-world situations (Donaldson 1978). Indeed, even Grade 12 students may benefit from thinking about $E = mc^2$ as a narrative compressed into an equation—and myth as a narrative form of scientific exploration.

# What Does a Narrative Look and Sound Like?

Although not all narratives look or sound like the narrative typical of a sports match (see fig. 1.1), they share similar conventions, such as beginning with a setting that includes time, people, and location. Some of these conventions are signaled as subheadings in figure 1.1. You may like to discuss this model and a range of other narratives, such as biographies, historical novels, and sports articles, with students and encourage them to identify the conventions.

---

## The North-South Game

**The Beginning** *(Who, What, When, Where)*

Fans who attended the annual North versus South soccer match at 2:10 P. M. on Saturday, September 25, at the Bakers Field Reserve witnessed a spectacular game.

**Event One** *(Statement plus Description plus Comment)*

The first five minutes set the tone for the whole game. Both teams held formation well and retained position. However, North showed their determination to win by demonstating their ability to win back the ball. Further, North showed they intended to make the ball do the work by using short, well-placed passes to take them up to the goal box. They were rewarded in the fifth minute when Jones launched a magnificent long-range shot that found the back of the net.

**Event Two** *(Statement plus Description plus Comment)*

South was content to defend and push forward on the counterattack. Their only goal scoring chance came when they played a long ball over the back of the North defense for the South forwards to run with and for Denise to run home in spectatcular, if not frustrated, fashion.

**The End**

It was a game of one side willing to attack and use their technical ability and of the other side content to defend and counterattack. The North-South Cup went North by three well-planned goals to one opportunistic goal.

---

*Figure 1.1*

SkyLight Training and Publishing Inc.

The conventions of this type of writing, including the event structure and use of the past tense, may not be entirely obvious to students, especially to less able readers and writers. Although it is important that students have some frame in which to write and think narratives, this should never be entirely prescriptive. Breaking the conventions, or combining two sets of conventions, can have stunning effects, as shown in the movie *Butch Cassidy and the Sundance Kid,* which combines the conventions of comedy and Western writing.

The Statement plus Description plus Comment, written beside events in figure 1.1, simply means that the paragraph might begin with a statement, such as The first five minutes set the tone for the whole match; followed by a description, Both teams held formation well and retained position; and completed with a comment, However, North showed their determination to win by demonstrating . . . . We see other ways of organizing paragraphs or series of paragraphs when we consider thinking and writing descriptions, reports, and arguments and discussions.

There are at least three types of narratives: personal, factual, and imaginative. Some general examples of these types are shown here:

Personal Narratives

- Diary, perhaps beginning with a sentence starter such as On Monday, I (or we) . . . or Yesterday, I . . .

- Journal or log of activities

Factual Narratives

- Narrative about a direct experience, such as a play presented by a senior class or a trip to a local shop

- Written observation about some event seen in the school yard (Encourage students to work in pairs and observe the same event, perhaps over a lunch break, and then tell about it. Have them compare their narratives.)

- Written account of an event that occurred at home, which might be shared with members of the family

- News story about an event that the local newspaper is likely to cover

Imaginative Narratives

- Adventure story about the life of a bear or a dinosaur

- Narrative outlining a day in the life of a drop of blood or an ozone molecule

- Written narrative about voyaging with Christopher Columbus

# How Do We Start Thinking and Writing Narratives?

## What Are Narrative Writing Frames?

Quite simply, a frame is a structure for holding something in a predetermined shape. There are two types of frames that help students structure their narrative writing: narrative writing frames and narrative thinking frames. Each will be discussed separately.

A narrative writing frame (see fig. 1.2) provides learners with a shape for draft writing of narrative text. The shape is signaled by subheadings that prompt students to think about some of the conventions of this type of writing. Writing frames are not designed to usurp the writing process, but rather to support it.

### Using the Narrative Writing Frame

Writing frames are used for draft writing by students who are unfamiliar with the conventions of narratives. The frame acts like a coat hook on which students can hang ideas as they write.

Narratives drafted using figure 1.2 (or the news story writing frame, to be introduced next) are likely to be well-structured, but devoid of authenticity, style, and a writer's voice. These characteristics of good writing tend to emerge when students revise, edit, confer, and act on other students' responses to their writing.

The narrative writing and news story writing frames are designed to help students draft their ideas, but students will still need assistance composing a beginning that flows rather than one that lists a series of who, why, where, when, and what statements in pedestrian fashion. Again, although the writing frame provides a structure in which to record a series of events, students will need help to link these events. After students have completed an initial draft on the frame, remind them that they are writing for an audience and that the audience needs to be engaged and encouraged to read on from the first sentence.

## What Is the News Story Writing Frame?

The Morning Talk is an institution in most Grade 1 and 2 classes. These talks contrast with the show-and-tell talk that usually involves description rather than narration. Figure 1.3 shows a model of a news story that might be presented during a Morning Talk. Morning Talks usually narrate events of recent importance to the speaker. In addition to the who, where, and when (the setting in other narratives), the why and what tell listeners and readers about an event and the reasons for its occurrence. The news story writing frame also includes comment, in the same way that reflection or the moral occurs in other narratives.

# Narrative Writing Frame

The purpose of a narrative is to record something that happened. *I* or *we* can be used in a personal narrative. If writing a narrative about what someone else did, use *he, she,* or *they*.

The title of my narrative might be _____

## Beginning

Write a paragraph that says who took part in the event, when and where the event took place, and why and how the event took place.

_____

_____

_____

## Middle (Events)

Write about the things that happened. Use the past tense. One way to write a paragraph is to start with a statement of what happened, add a more detailed description of what happened, and then include a comment. Useful words or phrases to introduce each event include *First, Then, Next, After that, Finally, Later,* and *The next day.*

_____

_____

_____

_____

_____

_____

## End

Write a concluding paragraph that restates the who, when, where, why, and how, and add a comment.

_____

_____

_____

_____

_____

*Figure 1.2*

SkyLight Training and Publishing Inc.

| Model News Story | | | | |
|---|---|---|---|---|
| **When?** Last night, after Dad got home from work, | **Who?** my Dad and I | **Where?** went up town to the Big Circle Bike Shop | **What?** to buy a BMX bike | **Why?/Comment** because next Saturday is my birthday and I can't wait to ride it. |

*Figure 1.3*

The news story writing frame (fig. 1.4) enables groups or individual students to draft their news story prior to presentation to the class.

### Using the News Story Writing Frame

The model in figure 1.4 is designed to help students to include all the parts usually found in a newspaper story. These parts are explicitly listed in question form to prompt writers to use the news story writing frame.

### How to Introduce the News Story Writing Frame

Typically, teachers will organize students into Morning Talk groups and ask each student to share a piece of news. (Students need to be alerted to this task the previous day.) Students use the frame to note what they might say under each heading before sharing their news.

An alternative to writing in the frame is for students to draw sketches, which they may refer to as they present their news story. After the talks, students use the news story writing frames to help them write.

## Assessing and Reflecting on Narrative Writing Frames

To assist teachers in monitoring and recording students progress, a narrative writing assessment rubric is provided (see fig. 1.5). Because the rubric clearly identifies objectives and performance standards, teachers may share the content with students after they have been introduced to the writing frames.

Although summative assessments (i.e., assessing where each student is right now) will be required from time to time, the focus in the assessment rubrics presented here is on formative assessment, using continuums in the form of arrows. Any assessment placed at the left end of the arrow indicates the student is still dependent on the teacher to achieve this behavior. An assessment placed at the right end indicates the student is consistently independent in achieving this behavior. Teachers may choose to date their observations on the arrows when they see examples of specific behaviors.

# News Story Writing Frame

The title of my news story might be_____

**When did it happen?**

_____

_____

**Who created the news?**

_____

_____

**Where did the news happen?**

_____

_____

**What happened?**

_____

_____

_____

_____

_____

**Why did it happen?**

_____

_____

_____

_____

**Comment**

_____

_____

_____

*Figure 1.4*

SkyLight Training and Publishing Inc.

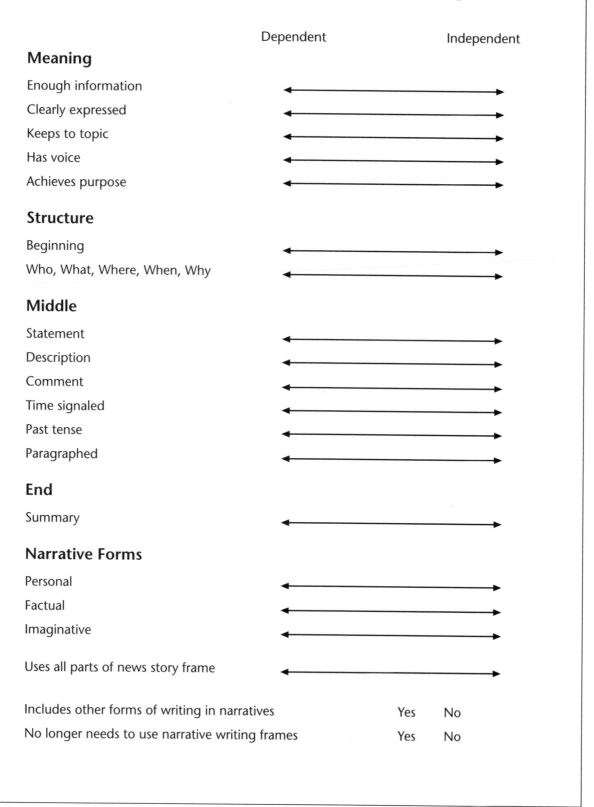

# Assessing Narrative Writing

|  | Dependent | Independent |
|---|---|---|

**Meaning**

Enough information

Clearly expressed

Keeps to topic

Has voice

Achieves purpose

**Structure**

Beginning

Who, What, Where, When, Why

**Middle**

Statement

Description

Comment

Time signaled

Past tense

Paragraphed

**End**

Summary

**Narrative Forms**

Personal

Factual

Imaginative

Uses all parts of news story frame

Includes other forms of writing in narratives     Yes     No

No longer needs to use narrative writing frames     Yes     No

*Figure 1.5*

SkyLight Training and Publishing Inc.

## What Are Narrative Thinking Frames?

The purpose of a narrative thinking frame is to help students prepare to talk or write narratives. These frames engage students in thinking to support the preparation of a narrative, in contrast to the kind of thinking required to compose, for example, an argument.

The following frames are designed to help students, prior to crafting a narrative, to think in clever and sometimes complex ways. These complex ways of thinking may not emerge naturally in the course of a student's development, but may require explicit introduction and practice.

These frames serve two audiences. Initially, they are used as teaching frameworks, that is, the teacher uses them to help students think and create narratives. Later, students use them independently. Two narrative thinking frames are described: the critical thinking frame and the timeline/excitement frame

# What Is the Critical Thinking Frame?

The purpose of critical thinking frames (fig. 1.6) is to improve the level of thinking associated with the average Morning Talk or written narrative. It is designed to be used in association with the news story and narrative writing frames. The thinking frame consists of a set of questions that add a critical dimension to narratives. They provide ways in which students can think critically about a newspaper article, an event in a history text, or a personal experience. It is expected that Grade 1 teachers might use the questions in the critical thinking frame during discussion, rewording them as required. Middle and upper grade teachers may provide the questions in written form for group or independent use. Upper grade students should also be challenged to create additional critical thinking questions (Lipman 1991).

## Using the Critical Thinking Frame

The critical thinking frame is used in conjunction with a news story writing frame, especially with students in the middle and senior grade levels. Typically, teachers use the critical thinking questions from the frame incidentally during discussion, especially in Grades 1 and 2, and well before making the questions explicit. When it is time to be explicit, it is best for the teacher to model one critical thinking question at a time—the one that seems most appropriate to the topic at hand. After all the questions have been modeled, the complete critical thinking frame can be introduced on paper. But, by age eight or so, students should be able to choose one or more questions from the critical thinking frame and use them while reading, writing, or preparing their narratives.

# Critical Thinking Frame

The event I am going to think about is _____

## Okay

Was it okay for this event to happen in our lifetime or in the past? Will it be okay for this event to happen again in the future?

_____

_____

_____

## Needed

Was the event needed?

_____

_____

_____

## Achieve

Did the event achieve its purpose?

_____

_____

_____

## Learn

What can we learn from what happened?

_____

_____

_____

## Change

How and why would you change what happened?

_____

_____

_____

*Figure 1.6*

## What Is a Timeline/Excitement Frame?

A timeline/excitement frame (fig. 1.7) encourages students to record dates, times, and events and to think critically about those events in written and visual form. The frame helps students, prior to writing, sequence events in words or pictures, using time signals. In short, the timeline/excitement frame helps students organize narratives sequentially and link events in the narrative.

### Using the Timeline/Excitement Frame

Teachers may begin using this frame by having students write the main events of an experience on cards and sort the cards in the order in which the events happened. Then, with the teacher's help, students decide how to signal when events took place and arrange this information in the frame. Signal words include

| last | during | after | at the same time |
|------|--------|-------|------------------|
| first | last week | when | before |
| later | on the second day | as soon as | next |

A graph is drawn within the frame indicating the excitement associated with each event (see fig. 1.7). One axis of the frame (usually the bottom axis) indicates time and the other axis represents excitement. An excitement scale is created, using either a numbered scale (1, dull, to 10, very exciting) or a word scale (incredibly boring to off the planet). These words may later find their way as comment into the written narrative. A graph line joining each event at their appropriate level of excitement provides a visual representation of the experience. The frame is completed with a picture and a written summary of each event.

Timeline/excitement frames, with key dates or other time signals, provide useful reading study guides. As readers find the dates or signals in the text, they can add in summary form (writing or sketches) the main event that occurred at that time.

## Assessing and Reflecting on Narrative Thinking Frames

Both the students' thinking and writing need to be assessed—by teacher and students. Figure 1.8 provides a rubric for assessing thinking in preparation for narrative writing. Introducing the assessment content to students is a good way to review and reinforce the major elements of each frame. Please note that some of the assessments on this rubric are introduced as practice activities in chapter 2.

# Model Timeline/Excitement Frame

**Main Events**          *Event 1*          *Event 2*          *Event 3*          *Event 4*

Picture of each event

**Excitement Graph**

*Excitement Levels*

Off the Planet

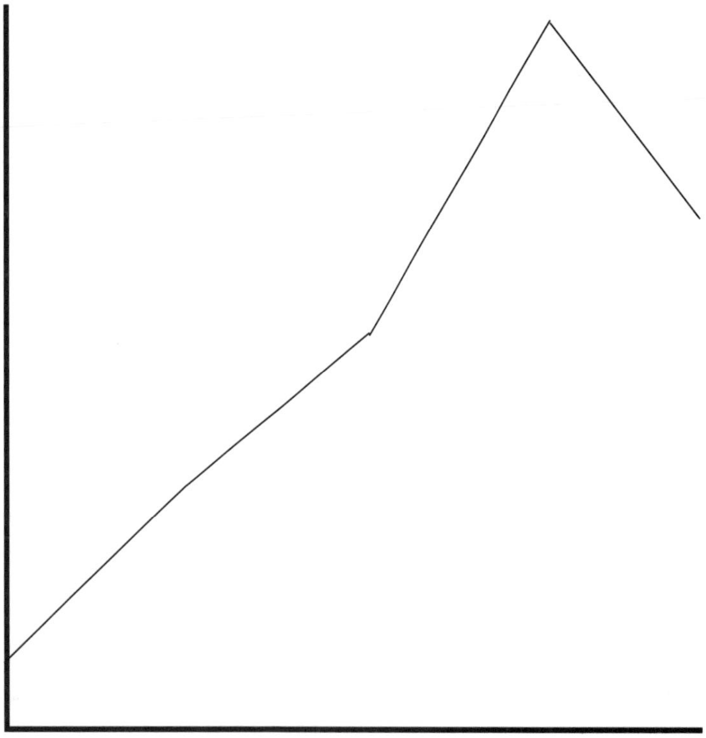

Boring

*Time Signals*          First…          After…          Later…          As the sun…

**Summary of Events**          . . . . . . . . .          . . . . . . . . .          . . . . . . . . .          . . . . . . . .

. . . . . . . . .          . . . . . . . . .          . . . . . . . . .          . . . . . . . .

. . . . . . . . .          . . . . . . . . .          . . . . . . . . .          . . . . . . . .

*Figure 1.7*

SkyLight Training and Publishing Inc.

# Assessing Narrative Thinking

|                                                                 | Dependent | Independent |
|-----------------------------------------------------------------|:---------:|:-----------:|
| Decides on purpose                                              | ←————————→ |
| Determines audience                                             | ←————————→ |
| **Narrative Writing Frame**                                     |           |             |
| Joint construction                                              | ←————————→ |
| Independent construction                                        | ←————————→ |
| **Timeline/Excitement Frame**                                   |           |             |
| Dates, labels, and details events on own timeline before writing | ←————————→ |
| Adds "excitement" graph to timeline                             | ←————————→ |
| **Critical Thinking Frame**                                     |           |             |
| Okay question                                                   | ←————————→ |
| Needed question                                                 | ←————————→ |
| Achieve question                                                | ←————————→ |
| Learn question                                                  | ←————————→ |
| Change question                                                 | ←————————→ |
| **Summarize-Pair-Share Activity**                               |           |             |
| Shares with partner                                             | ←————————→ |
| Shares with class                                               | ←————————→ |
| **Add, Zoom Activity**                                          |           |             |
| Adds                                                            | ←————————→ |
| Zooms                                                           | ←————————→ |
| Flashbacks                                                      | ←————————→ |
| Squeezes                                                        | ←————————→ |
| X-tends                                                         | ←————————→ |
| **Sketches, Murals, and Photographs**                           |           |             |
| Draws or sequences                                              | ←————————→ |
| Writes captions for pictures                                    | ←————————→ |
| Adds signal words                                               | ←————————→ |
| Uses to write narrative                                         | ←————————→ |

*Figure 1.8*

SkyLight Training and Publishing Inc.

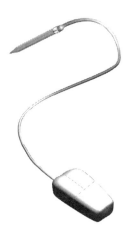

# PRACTICE ACTIVITIES
## to Support Thinking and Writing Narratives

CHAPTER 2

## Oral Language Activities

**Focus Activity** 

# Action Cards

**Add, Zoom, Flashback, Squeeze, and X-tend action cards** are prompts to help students think about an event before they write it as a narrative. Each prompt requires a different way of thinking about the event.

- *Add* helps students practice the skill of recalling events in sequence.

- *Zoom* helps students practice the skill of inferring what happened during and between events.

- *Flashback* helps students practice the skill of self-correction and checking.

- *Squeeze* helps students practice the skill of summarization.

- *X-tend* helps students practice the active listening skill of prediction—what might happen next in the narrative.

**Objective**

This activity is designed to extend understanding about narratives in nonthreatening ways. Specifically, in respect to narratives, it helps students recall, draw inferences, and summarize. In respect to classroom management

- Flashback allows less able students to hear the text again and to repeat again the contributions of other students.

- X-tend allows early finishing groups to continue working while other groups complete the recall and provides an opportunity for them to share their additional events with the class.

## Input

Students are presumed to have played a simplified version of this activity several times before playing this more extensive activity. Perhaps each card was introduced individually during shorter, less structured mini-activities. Each group of students needs a set of action cards. The set consists of the following verbs and descriptions:

- Add—When you pick up this card, continue retelling the narrative from where the last person stopped, or if you are the first player, begin retelling.

- Zoom—When you pick up this card, zoom in on the last thing said and describe it in detail. You may include things that were not stated in the narrative.

- Flashback—When you pick up this card, go back to any part of the narrative already retold and continue retelling. This will give you a chance to say things that were left out by a previous speaker.

- Squeeze—When you pick up this card, summarize in one sentence everything that has been retold so far.

- X-tend—When you pick up this card, add another part or chapter to the narrative.

When beginning to use this activity, give groups only one action card at a time, so that the named action is clearly understood. It might take several sessions to set up the full set of actions for the activity. The Add card should be demonstrated first, then the Flashback, Squeeze, and Zoom cards, followed finally by the X-tend card.

Each group also needs a copy of the text. For younger students, a picture book at the average (or below) reading level of the class is preferred. The book should be open on the desk as the students play the activity.

## Procedure

1. Form students into groups of five or six and ask them to sit around a table. Give each group a copy of the text to follow.

2. Select a short story or narrative with a clear structure that will be meaningful to the students. (The text might be related to a current theme of study.) Read the story to the students or along with students as they follow the text.

3. Give each group a set of instruction cards. Explain that each card has a different keyword instruction and a short description of the instruction. (Depending on the experience of the class, an instruction set may include some or all of the action instructions.) Explain the following game rules:

   a. Any card on the table may be picked up and used.

   b. Cards may be reused.

   c. The X-tend card is used at the very end and signals that the narrative is complete.

   d. The student holding the card is the only one allowed to speak.

4. After the narrative has been read, select a student (the tallest, for instance) in each group to pick up the Add card and begin retelling the narrative. Explain that when the first student finishes, he or she should place the Add card back on the table. Another group member should then pick up another card, and so on. Remind students not to use the X-tend card until the narrative has been completely recalled. (The activity proceeds by students successively picking cards that direct them to variously add, flashback, and so forth.)

## Metacognitive Discussion

1. What kind of thinking did the Zoom card make you do?

2. What was said by students in your group that was not said in the narrative? What kind of thinking did they do?

3. Which card was the most interesting to use? What made it interesting? What kind of thinking did this card prompt you to do?

4. Did the cards help you prepare for writing? What have you learned about preparing to write that you could use at another time?

5. What was said by students who used the Squeeze card? What kind of thinking did they do? When would you use this kind of thinking?

## Closure

Share what was said in response to the X-tend card. Set goals for improving response to particular cards.

**Focus Activity**  # Summarize-Pair-Share

In the **summarize-pair-share** activity, students practice summarizing and rehearsing events orally before writing a narrative. The summaries may be shared with the class or a peer, thus assisting all students prior to writing their narratives.

### Objective

Summarize-pair-share fosters active listening, giving students a purpose for listening. Some form of rehearsal usually precedes draft writing. This activity provides a nonthreatening opportunity to rehearse an event that students may later record as a written narrative. The activity also aids in the development of oral fluency and quick thinking.

### Input

Prior to using this activity, students need to have read or shared a narrative or been on a school trip together. They also need to hear summaries, to compare summaries, and to make the word *summary* part of their thinking vocabulary.

### Procedure

1. Use this activity after a shared or read narrative of an experience. (Note: Using the activity too frequently while reading or retelling a shared experience tends to destroy the narrative and produce negative attitudes.)

2. Instruct students that they will be asked to summarize the events being presented and share the summary with a partner. The summary is to be approximately one sentence in length.

3. Read the narrative of one event to the class or ask the class to talk about a shared experience, limiting discussion to one event. Students will anticipate the task of producing an oral summary of the event and make mental notes of the important pieces.

4. Allow a brief silent pause so that students can mentally plan and rehearse their summary.

5. Signal the students to pair. Ask students to give a summary to their partners and encourage them to refine their single-sentence summaries as they talk. Then, instruct students from one, two, or all pairs to share their own or their partners' summary with the class. If time allows, lead students to vote for the best summary sentence and record the sentence on a timeline/excitement frame.

6. Repeat steps three through five for as many events as are reasonable.

## Metacognitive Discussion

1. What things did you leave out of your narrative summary?

2. What did you think about as the narrative was read?

3. Did telling your summary to a partner help?

4. How might summarize-pair-share help you write?

## Closure

Ask students to say in one sentence what they did during the activity and what they learned during the activity.

SkyLight Training and Publishing Inc.

**Focus Activity** # Commentary

The **commentary** activity asks students to give a running commentary about an activity being performed by another student.

## Objective

This is probably the easiest and most effective way to ease students into thinking and writing narratives. Specifically, students are asked to observe and describe an event in real time and in enough detail to make it clear to someone who is not watching.

## Input

Perhaps the easiest way to begin this activity is for a student to slowly perform a task and the teacher to model a running narrative. The students need to know that sufficient details are required—the test of which is to have them listen to, but not view, the task, then perform it themselves.

## Procedure

1. Group students in pairs and ask one student in each pair to perform—slowly—a simple task (such as drawing a square). Ask their partners to provide a continuous and detailed oral commentary of the action as it occurs. (This is a bit like calling the Kentucky Derby—you will have some students good at that kind of narrative as well.)

2. An alternative is to have the students mime an activity. If class members have shared an experience such as a trip to a cafeteria or an auto repair shop, they can mime something that happened during the trip while their partners provide running commentary.

## Metacognitive Discussion

1. What words did you use to start sentences that described each part of the task?

2. What were the differences between the more and less successful running narratives?

## Closure

Read a quality narrative (a famous work of fiction) that describes how something happened, for example, how Melville narrates the harpooning of a whale, or how Huckleberry Finn built a raft.

# Visual Language Activities

**Focus Activity** # Video Narration

The **video narration** activity is similar to the commentary activity in that students compose their own running commentary to accompany a video clip.

## Objective

This activity helps students explore the language of narration and to think critically about the original commentaries that accompany video clips. By comparing their commentary with the original, students rapidly appreciate bias, the type of language used, and the structure of this type of narrative, which can be contrasted with that of a written narrative.

## Input

Students need to know that the narrative that accompanies video differs in detail and in length from the running narrative that accompanies the description of a task. Often, what is said elaborates on the obvious and provides for pauses so that the visual text can speak for itself.

Prior to this activity, you might like to make an audiotape of a running narrative of a video clip—saying what can be seen happening—and play the audiotape with the video on mute. Then, play the video with its own soundtrack and compare the two narratives.

Narrative documentaries are popular on television. They range from a commentary associated with a sports game through a well-researched historical documentary, such as an incident during the Civil War. Television documentaries are also easy to come by in video format and provide great models for the students.

## Procedure

1. As a class, view a short video of a familiar event(s) with no sound.

2. Ask students work in small groups to orally compose, then write, a commentary to accompany the video clip action. Explain that this commentary should include both factual retelling and comment.

3. Instruct students to rehearse their commentaries. Ask each group to nominate one member to read the commentary as the videotape is played again with the sound off.

4. As a class, view the video with the sound on. Lead students to compare the original sound commentary with their commentary (language and content).

## Metacognitive Discussion

1. What were the differences between your group's narrative commentary and the video commentary?

2. What kind of narrative commentary works best?

3. How does this commentary differ from other types of narrative?

## Closure

Ask students to try this activity at home with a television program. They can turn off the sound and narrate it for their family or friends.

SkyLight Training and Publishing Inc.

**Focus Activity**

# Sketches and Murals

**Sketches and murals** involve students drawing or painting part (usually the best part) of a shared experience on large sheets of paper. Each drawing or sketch effectively summarizes an event. When put together, these visuals provide an overview of the shared experience. These pages, together with other students' work, tell the key aspects of an experience.

## Objective

Rehearsal and the visual elaboration of meaning are central to this activity. Some of the key vocabulary words students need when writing their own narratives can be noted during this activity.

## Input

This activity works well as a joint effort by a group of students who have shared a similar experience, such as a class trip. It may be expedient to delegate responsibility for specific events, so that all events related to the class experience are covered.

## Procedure

1. Arrange students in small groups of three or four.

2. Ask each group to draw a sketch of an event that occurred during a class trip or other shared experience.

3. Display the murals, in sequence by time, on the walls. Ask students to walk about and visit each mural, and, as a group, stand in front of one mural (not their own) that they would like to work with.

4. Ask groups to annotate their mural by

   a. Adding large captions underneath.

   b. Writing and inserting giant speech bubbles with appropriate comments to the mouths of people in the mural.

   c. Writing people's names by their figures and also adding the names of key features depicted in the mural.

   d. Adding words that connect one mural to the next.

## Metacognitive Discussion

1. How does drawing help you think about an event?

2. What is the difference between what you draw and what you say?

SkyLight Training and Publishing Inc.

**Closure**

1. Read all the captions, speech bubbles, and other text with the class.

2. Have students read their speech bubbles.

Closure

**Focus Activity**

# Photographs

The **photographs** activity involves preparing captions for photographs taken during a class experience. These photographs provide a rich source of information that can help students write their narratives when they return to class.

## Objective

Rehearsal and the visual elaboration of meaning are central to this activity. Some of the key vocabulary words students need when writing their own narratives can be noted during this activity.

## Input

Students need a series of photographs taken during the event to be written about.

## Procedure

1. There are several ways to organize a class so that the captions are of high quality.

   a. Work with the whole class. A student is chosen to dictate a final caption to the teacher after hearing suggestions from other students. As other students offer their suggestions, the teacher can make a temporary record of key vocabulary that might assist the appointed student.

   b. Work in small groups. Appoint a student in each group to be the recorder. Each student in the group should suggest a caption before the recorder creates a final version. (This works especially well with students in Grade 3 and above.)

2. Ask students to sequence the photographs and select one or two to work with.

3. Instruct students to discuss an event, jointly compose a caption, write it on a piece of paper, and place the caption with the photograph in a trip album.

4. You might also suggest that students cut out paper arrows with words indicating the passage of time and place the arrows in the album between photographs.

## Metacognitive Discussion

1. Note how each student brings a slightly different perspective to each photograph.

2. Discuss the strengths of group construction.

3. Note the role of words that signal the passage of time.

4. Note that a quality text includes reflections in addition to a narrative of events.

**Closure**

As an alternative to a visual experience, read a text with students and record that narrative on an audiocassette for use at a listening post, a preassigned station in the classroom that is associated with the event.

SkyLight Training and Publishing Inc.

# Written Language Activities

**Focus Activity** 

# Round-Robin Narration

In the **round-robin narration** activity, each student writes a narrative of a shared event, then passes the written narrative to another student, who adds to it.

### Objective

The purpose of this activity is for students to jointly construct a narrative, to understand coherence and cohesion in text, and to recall a shared event.

### Input

Students witness the same event, such as a baseball game.

### Procedure

1. Arrange students in small groups of four to six.

2. Ask each person in the group to begin writing a narrative of the event. They may work for three to five minutes.

3. When the time is up, signal each person to pass their papers to the right. Explain that each person should read what has been written, edit if necessary, and continue the narrative by writing for another three to five minutes.

4. Continue this round robin until each person in the group has contributed to the narrative. Explain that the last person has the task of completing the narrative and doing the final edit.

### Metacognitive Discussion

1. What did you have to do before continuing the narrative? What does this tell you about the process of writing?

2. What are the advantages and disadvantages of composing a narrative in this way?

### Closure

Return the papers to the first writer and allow them to silently read the papers. Students discuss sections of the text with various original authors.

**Focus Activity**      # Read and Retell

**Read and retell** asks students to retell a narrative that they have heard.

### Objective

Read and retell is primarily a means of assessing students' knowledge of the structure and meaning of narratives. The read and retell activity can form part of an assessment portfolio for each student.

### Input

The teacher reads a narrative to or along with students.

### Procedure

1. Ask students, in pairs or independently, to do one of the following:

   a. Retell the story or narrative to a partner.

   b. Rewrite as much of the narrative as possible.

   c. Draw a series of sketches that retell the event.

2. Ask students to share and discuss with the class. In the discussion, direct students to focus on

   a. the information omitted,

   b. the use of words to signal the passage of time,

   c. the use of past tense.

### Metacognitive Discussion

1. Did we all retell, rewrite, and draw the same thing? Why not?

2. What was retold, rewritten, or drawn that was not in the original text? What kind of thinking is involved here?

### Closure

Allow students to share written and visual texts. Ask students to label sections of their texts as beginning, events (or middle), and end.

**Focus Activity** # Narrative Reconstruction

**Narrative reconstruction** requires students to rebuild a familiar narrative from its pieces.

## Objective

This activity is designed to help students further develop their understanding of the structure and content of narratives by physically manipulating chunks of narrative text.

## Input

The teacher selects and photocopies a clearly and logically sequenced narrative. The text is then cut up into the beginning, the events, and the end. Students are presented with these logical pieces of the narrative and reconstruct the original narrative from them.

## Procedure

1. Allow students to work in groups first, then work individually. Explain that students are to reconstruct the text by pasting the pieces back together in sequence.

2. Ask students to share their reconstructions with the rest of the class. Students should identify the clues in the text that helped them put the text in sequence.

## Metacognitive Discussion

1. What clues did you use when reconstructing the text?

2. How could the author have made the text easier to reconstruct?

## Closure

Extend this activity by asking students to reconstruct the text on large sheets of paper, leaving spaces between each event. Then, challenge students to write an additional event in a space. As an alternative, remove an event and challenge students to jointly write a replacement.

**Focus Activity**    # Text Elaboration

**Text elaboration** asks students to expand on a beginning narrative sentence about a familiar event.

## Objective

Text elaboration is designed to focus attention on the kind of statements, usually located at the beginning of a paragraph, that describe some event in a narrative. It helps students develop the description embedded in these paragraphs.

## Input

The class shares an experience, such as a short trip around the school grounds.

## Procedure

1. Begin by stating or writing a simple sentence of fact, such as First, we walked out of the classroom.

2. Ask students to elaborate on the sentence with details and comments. For example they might say, "We walked out of the woodworking class. It was a class that no one ever liked." Allow a minute or two for this elaboration.

3. Continue to provide simple starter sentences for the next events, such as Next, we walked across the school yard. Continue until all events in the experience have been considered.

## Metacognitive Discussion

1. What was it about the starter sentences that helped us construct the narrative?

2. What other starter sentences could we use?

## Closure

Encourage students to write a narrative of one or more events in the experience, either jointly or independently.

**Focus Activity** # Change of Person

The **change of person** activity asks students to rewrite a text from the third person into the first person, changing the point of view.

## Objective

A convention of most narratives is the use of the third person. This activity is designed to focus students' attention on the use of this tense and the first person, which is typical of personal narratives or autobiographies. A key objective is helping students appreciate the points of view possible when using the third person and the first person and how the selected point of view enables the narrator to create different meanings.

## Input

The teacher provides a narrative written in the third person. The narrative may be one that students have written before or may be a short narrative from literature (a work of fiction).

## Procedure

1. Ask students to rewrite in the first person a narrative written in the third person. That is, they are to change the text to read as if the writer were experiencing the event.

2. Instruct students to share their rewritten version with a friend.

## Metacognitive Discussion

1. How does the narrative differ when it is written in the first person?

2. Does the event itself seem different if it is told in the first person?

## Closure

Ask students to swap papers (they need the original and the version written with a different point of view). Ask students to share insights and new meaning with the class.

**Focus Activity** # Inserting Narrative Signal Words

**Inserting narrative signal words** is a cloze activity designed to focus students attention on the use of words key to depicting a narrative clearly and concisely.

## Objective

A convention of most narratives is the use of specific signal words that clearly flag the sequence of actions. This activity emphasizes these words as it alerts students to their value in forming a clear narrative.

## Input

The teacher copies a well-structured narrative with clear signal words or phrases, such as Next . . . , The following day . . . , Later . . . , and so forth. The teacher deletes the signal words, leaving a space for the students to write. Deleted words, together with some additional words, are listed at the bottom of the page of text.

## Procedure

1. Ask students to work in pairs or individually for this activity.

2. Give each student a copy of the narrative with blank spaces in the text.

3. Ask students to fill in the blanks using the words at the bottom of the page. Tell them that there are extra words, that no word may be used twice, and that they are to put the best word in each blank space.

4. Direct students to share their choices for each blank space and discuss their cloze insertions. Pay particular attention to answering the question, Are these the best words to use?

5. Provide students with the original script, with the deleted words in place and marked with a highlighter.

## Metacognitive Discussion

1. Might these words only occur in a narrative or might they be used elsewhere?

2. Discuss situations where students have used different words in the blanks—is there a best choice?

## Closure

Encourage students to make a poster display of signal words.

SkyLight Training and Publishing Inc.

**Focus Activity**

# Separating Fact From Comment

The **separating fact from comment** activity asks students to distinguish between factual statements and those that are commentary added by the author.

## Objective

Narratives are never purely factual texts; opinions find their way into most writing. This activity focuses on the personal comment that is found in narratives. This activity helps students distinguish fact from opinion and helps them appreciate the role of opinion (bias) in narrative.

## Input

Students are given a narrative that contains comment. Initially, it may be easier for students if the text is presented sentence by sentence, for example,

> On Monday we went to the museum show in town. (Fact)
>
> We went on the bus. (Fact)
>
> The driver went too fast. (Comment)
>
> We saw big mirrors at the show. (Fact)
>
> The mirror made me look fat. (Fact)
>
> The best part in the show was the earthquake building. (Comment)

## Procedure

1. Group students in pairs.

2. Instruct students to read the text and underline sections of text that are factual in one color and those that are comment in another color.

3. Ask students to respond to the comments. (For example, you might ask, "Did the driver go too fast?" or "Was the earthquake building the best part?")

## Metacognitive Discussion

1. How do we distinguish the factual sentences from the comment sentences?

2. Were there special words that helped us identify the two types of sentences?

3. Are there signal words for comments?

4. Why would you want to distinguish fact from comment anyway?

5. What is the value of recognizing fact and comment in a text?

**Closure**

Ask students to make up statements and have the class determine whether they are fact or opinion. (For example, Michael Jackson is the greatest living dancer.)

# WRITING Narratives

CHAPTER 3

## Introduction to the Narrative Writing Model Program

The focus activities in this chapter are planned around a model program for introducing narrative writing. After an introduction to the program, which presents the objectives, context, and teacher preparation, individual activities are presented sequentially to show an example of a coherent program.

Briefly, the model program for narrative texts is a unit about people that help us. It is designed for Grades 1 and 2. The context of the study is a civics unit focusing on the students' school. The particular event is a trip to the cafeteria. The types of thinking that are developed are sequencing, recalling, evaluating, composing bias, identifying patterns over time, composing cause and effect, inferencing, generalizing, and linking. The specific objectives of the program are shown below.

The oral language objectives are to help students

1. talk clearly to small groups about their experiences;
2. recall and organize events that occurred during the experience;
3. listen to speakers and identify how their narratives were structured;
4. listen to speakers and recall the content of what was shared;
5. interact with others in small groups;
6. piggyback on previous speakers, that is, repeat an idea from a previous speaker before adding their own narratives.

The exploring language objectives are to help students

1. explore the language choices made by the authors of narratives;

2. identify the common conventions of a narrative, including the use of past tense;

3. use a news story thinking frame prior to presenting an oral narrative;

4. use a narrative writing frame to jointly and independently construct a narrative.

The narrative thinking objectives are to help students

1. construct a timeline/excitement frame prior to writing;

2. use a critical thinking frame prior to composing oral and written narratives.

To prepare for this unit, teachers need to

1. Arrange with the manager of the school cafeteria or a local restaurant for a class visit. (Later, the teacher should give the manager a short list of the questions that students might ask.)

2. Organize teacher's aides and parents to assist during the field trip to the cafeteria.

3. Borrow a camera, check for film, and be clear on operating procedures.

4. Borrow a video camera and assign a teacher's aide to tape the field trip.

5. Be prepared to supply paper and paints or crayons for students to create pictures and written texts.

   a. Cut out large paper arrows for later use between pictures.

   b. Prepare an overhead transparency of a model narrative.

   c. Photocopy the news story and narrative writing frames from this part of the book.

   d. Photocopy the critical thinking frames.

The focus activities presented in this chapter are designed as a set of linked activities, to be given over a period of time. As a reminder that an activity might depend upon another activity, session numbers are added. Linkage is particularly likely with the activities in the sections on working with writing and thinking frames.

# Building Knowledge of the Topic

**Focus Activity**

# Cafeteria Visit

The **cafeteria visit** is the actual event that is to be shared by the students and serves as the basis for their written narratives. The visit involves doing what the narrative will retell. (Session 1)

**Objective**

Students acquire new knowledge about a topic before writing, develop an understanding of the workings of the cafeteria, practice interview skills, and construct a narrative of the event.

**Input**

The teacher has arranged a visit to the cafeteria.

**Procedure**

During the visit, ask students to do a number of things that will become the events in the narrative.

1. Ask students to interview the cafeteria manager.

2. Direct students to view a demonstration of food preparation or serving equipment.

3. Encourage students to become involved in one of the cafeteria's functions.

4. Tell students to discuss ongoing events. Ask them to use the names of equipment in the cafeteria. Ongoing narratives of what they have done and seen so far could use language pattern starters, such as First, we . . . , After we looked at the . . . , Next we . . . , And then . . . , as situated memory aids for recall. During this discussion and later, back in the classroom, collect and combine students' initial responses so that the length and quality of what they say is extended.

**Metacognitive Discussion**

1. Are there any changes we might make in how we interviewed the cafeteria manager?

2. How did our initial responses change after we thought a bit more about what we had said?

**Closure**

Ask students to draw a picture of one event and write a caption.

**Focus Activity**

# Verbal Rehearsal

**Verbal rehearsal** of the shared experience gives students a time to remember specific events, as well as the opportunity to use sequence words and share the event with others. (Session 2)

### Objective

This activity helps students to reinforce and recall specific events in oral discussion before writing about them.

### Input

Students have shared a trip to the cafeteria and will be writing about that experience.

### Procedure

1. Instruct students to work in groups of five or six.

2. Ask students to describe the part of the trip they liked best and to make up a title for their best part, such as Rolling the Pastry. Record these titles on the board.

3. Invite the whole class to act out selected experiences, with students talking about what they dramatize—acting as commentators for the action.

4. Ask students to jointly or individually write narratives of the event.

### Metacognitive Discussion

1. What difficulties did you encounter when you were acting as commentators?

2. How does the language of an oral commentary differ from that of a written narrative?

### Closure

Invite the class to read written narratives and give responses to authors. Work as a class to design a checklist for event narratives.

**Focus Activity** # Visual Rehearsal

**Visual rehearsal** of the shared experience involves students drawing or painting an event from the visit. (Session 3)

## Objective

This activity helps students to reinforce and recall specific events visually before writing about them.

## Input

As a class, students recall and identify events of the shared experience.

## Procedure

1. Arrange students in groups of three to five members.

2. Before beginning, ask each group to choose one event, their "best part" from the visit that will be the subject of their illustration.

3. Encourage groups to represent their chosen "best part" in some visual form, using paints or crayons. Suggest that students might like to label the names of people and equipment in their picture or to add giant speech bubbles coming from people's mouths, showing what was described or asked. (Labels and speech bubbles can be attached with temporary adhesive tape for later removal when students write their narratives.)

## Metacognitive Discussion

1. How did drawing the experience affect your understanding of that experience?

2. How might drawing help us understand ideas or experiences in other subjects?

## Closure

Display the art on the wall, allowing the students to determine the sequence for the display.

# Modeling Narratives

 **Focus Activity** # Modeling an Oral Narrative

**Modeling an oral narrative** provides students with the opportunity to hear narratives being read by the teacher. (Session 4)

---

### Objective

This gives the teacher the opportunity to model oral narratives before students begin writing.

---

### Input

The teacher chooses several short narratives that can be read aloud and that contain clear representations of the narrative features of text.

---

### Procedure

1. Read a narrative aloud.

2. Repeat step one with the same narrative, this time interrupting to identify and explain the structure, tense, and use of signal words as they occur in the text.

3. Read another narrative aloud. This time, ask students to join in identifying the key parts of the narrative. For example, ask one group to listen for the beginning of events, another group to listen for the end of events, and a third group to listen for the signal words that are used. Ask groups to signal by raising their hands or standing up when their feature occurs. Interrupt the reading to discuss what they have to say. Get comments from other students.

---

### Metacognitive Discussion

1. How did we recognize the beginning of an event? the end of an event?

2. How did signal words help you understand the narrative?

---

### Closure

Direct each group to report how difficult their task was and how they were able to do it anyway.

# Working With Narrative Thinking Frames

**Focus Activity**

# Timeline/Excitement Frame

Using a **timeline/excitement frame** helps students organize events in a narrative before writing about it. (Session 5)

## Objective

This activity helps students to recognize an appropriate flow and the type of information needed for a narrative.

## Input

The teacher needs an enlarged, bare-bones outline of the timeline/excitement frame (the format shown in figure 1.7 but without actual content), paper for writing captions, and a piece of string. Students need a shared experience to serve as content. If time is short, students may use drawings and captions from earlier activities, if they are available. Students may have been introduced to the timeline/excitement frame separately, or this activity may serve as the introduction.

## Procedure:

1. Ask students to draw a series of sketches depicting the events. (This step may have been done separately. Also, photographs may be used for visual representation with the timeline/excitement frame.)

2. Direct students to sequence their drawings (or photographs taken during the trip).

3. Invite students to place the drawings on the timeline/ excitement frame across the top of the graph, following the heading Main Events, to form a timeline showing the events in time sequence.

4. Tell students to jointly compose summary captions for each event pictured, with one student acting as recorder. (This step may have been done separately.) Students place the captions below the timeline/excitement graph, across from the heading Summary of Events and in line with the picture of the event on the top of the chart.

5. Ask students to jointly compose time signals to use as the scale on the time axis (usually the horizontal axis), print them on paper, and place them along the axis with appropriate spacing.

6. Instruct students to jointly compose an excitement scale to use on the excitement level axis (usually the vertical axis). The scale may be either numeric, such as 0 for boring to 10 for perfect, or words that indicate a range, such as totally awful to perfectly wonderful. Students print the words or numbers on paper tags and place them on the axis at appropriate spacing.

7. Beginning with the first event, ask students to determine the excitement level and attach a string to the chart at that point. Instruct them to continue until each event is represented. The string will form a line that visually replays the excitement ebb and flow for the experience. The higher the string goes, the more exciting the event was seen to be.

An alternative to reviewing each event in sequence is to use a human graph activity. Ask students to stand by the drawing of the event that they found most exciting. Use the size of the crowd for each event to give a relative indication of event excitement. That is, the picture attracting the largest number of students is most exciting, the picture with the next largest number of students is the next most exciting, down the line to the one with no students. Then, direct students to convert the relative indicator (i.e., the number of people) to a point on the scale, with the largest number of people representing the highest level of excitement, and so on.

## Metacognitive Discussion

1. What do you notice about the structure of narratives?

2. Why are narratives structured this way?

3. Do the events need to be in the order they are displayed on the graph?

## Closure

Ask students to take one summary and expand it and to construct a wall display. Direct students to complete a new timeline/excitement frame with a different narrative and compare the two.

**Focus Activity** # Critical Thinking Frame

The **critical thinking frame** activity introduces the frame and asks students to review a particular activity or event in terms of the critical thinking frame questions. (Session 6)

## Objective

This activity assists students in reviewing and evaluating an experience in terms of value and accomplishment.

## Input

Students need a shared experience to use as the content of this exercise. This activity may be used to introduce the critical thinking frame itself, but it is best if students have been exposed to the questions in the frame informally during discussion and previous activities. An enlarged copy of the frame is displayed for easy viewing.

## Procedure

1. Explain why thinking about events and experiences in critical or evaluative terms is an important part of preparing to write about them. Introduce the critical thinking frame and examine and discuss each question with the students.

2. Arrange students in groups of four to six.

3. Instruct each group to select an event associated with the experience.

4. Tell groups to examine their events, using the critical thinking frame.

## Metacognitive Discussion

1. Could we apply these questions to another topic or subject?

2. How did your thinking about the event change as a result of this activity?

3. Why should we think critically?

## Closure

Ask each group to share its reflections about this activity with the class.

# Working with Narrative Writing Frames

**Focus Activity**     # Modeling a Written Narrative

**Modeling a written narrative** introduces the narrative writing frame and presents a model of a narrative for students to review. (Session 7)

### Objective

The teacher models written narratives before students begin writing. Students identify and apply the conventions of written narratives.

### Input

The teacher introduces the narrative writing frame, models written narratives, and explains the structure and tense that are used.

### Procedure

1. Read a short quality narrative to the students.

2. Discuss and refresh students' memories of a recent shared experience, such as a cafeteria visit.

3. Model how the narrative writing frame can be used to record the visit.

   a. Point to each subheading on the frame and provide an oral narrative

   b. Demonstrate how to draft a written narrative within the frame using a think-aloud procedure. For example, you might say, "Now, the first event was . . . I'll put it under event one . . . and use the past tense . . . ."

### Metacognitive Discussion

Ask groups to discuss the following questions:

1. How might a narrative frame help us write our drafts?

2. What did I (the teacher) have to think about while writing my draft narrative?

### Closure

Ask groups to report on their results from discussing the metacognitive questions.

**Focus Activity** Linking Events

**Linking events** is an activity that allows students to discover and use signal words and conjunction phrases to connect pictures or drawings of different events in a narrative. (Session 8)

### Objective

This activity reinforces the recall and use of signal words and phrases.

### Input

Students have a shared experience to serve as the content of the writing exercise and are familiar with the narrative writing frame and its requirements. The teacher displays pictures, either drawings or photographs, of the experience so that the students can see them.

### Procedure

1. Instruct students to construct signal words and phrases to go with the pictures of each event that occurred during the experience. These words should include introductory and ending words and phrases as well as linkage cues.

2. Ask students to print signal words and phrases on paper labels and place them appropriately on the displayed event pictures.

3. Invite students to print signal words and phrases on paper arrows and place the arrows so that an appropriate signal word or phrase links two pictures.

### Metacognitive Discussion

1. Students critically assess the choice of signal word and phrases and suggest alternatives.

2. Students discuss the effect of replacing signal words and phrases with numbers.

### Closure

Have students read the narrative from the labels and pictures, thus reinforcing the event sequence.

**Focus Activity** Jointly Writing a Narrative

**Jointly writing a narrative** gives students an opportunity to collaborate as a class on producing a narrative. (Session 9)

## Objective

This activity develops familiarity with the narrative writing frame.

## Input

Students have a shared experience that serves as the content for the writing exercise and have been introduced to the narrative writing frame.

## Procedure

1. Review with the students how to use the narrative writing frame.

2. Lead students to jointly construct part of the cafeteria narrative using the frame. Guide students as they work.

## Metacognitive Discussion

What do you feel the frame may stop you from doing that would be helpful in making meaning? For example, does it stop you from inserting a poem or scientific explanation into the event narrative?

## Closure

Discuss the following questions with the class:

1. What do we need to do better?

2. What could we say when responding to an author's narrative?

**Focus Activity** # Writing a Narrative Together

**Writing a narrative together** gives students the opportunity to write as a group, thus sharing the task of telling about the shared event. (Session 10)

## Objective

Students apply knowledge of narratives and their skill in using narrative frames to jointly construct a text. They identify and recognize how audience determines the choice of words and meanings in a narrative. They critically assess whether the narrative achieved the author's purpose.

## Input

Students need a shared experience to use for content, and they need to be familiar with the narrative writing frame.

## Procedure

1. Discuss audience and purpose for the writing exercise with the class and choose the most appropriate narrative type for the purpose.

2. Arrange students in small groups of four to six. Ask each group to choose an event from the shared experience to write about.

3. Ask students to write a narrative about the event, using the narrative writing frame as a basis and keeping in mind the audience and purpose chosen by the class. Allow ten minutes for this activity.

## Metacognitive Discussion

1. Did the narrative frame help you compose your narrative?

2. What language choices did you make in consideration of the audience?

3. When do you feel you could dispense with the frame?

## Closure

Invite groups to share their drafts with other groups or the whole class.

**Focus Activity** # Writing a Narrative Independently

**Writing a narrative independently** asks students to prepare narratives on their own about a shared activity. (Session 11)

**Objective**

Students practice writing narratives.

**Input**

Students individually choose an experience to write about; they need to be familiar with both narrative writing frames and appropriate thinking frames.

**Procedure**

1. Lead students to identify their purpose for writing this particular narrative, for example, to share with parents or caregivers or with another class, to record personal events, or so forth.

2. Ask students to determine their audience and how that audience might affect how and what they write.

3. Instruct students to independently write their narratives, depending on their skill level, using one of the following methods:

   a. Ask students to write drafts on scraps of paper, then talk with you before composing their written text.

   b. Ask less skilled students to work in groups with you, jointly constructing a draft using the narrative writing frame.

   c. Ask students to complete sentences using signal word or phrase starters you supply, such as During a trip to the cafeteria . . . or During activities following the experience . . . .

   d. Ask fluent writers to compose their narratives independently.

4. Work with students one-on-one or direct students to work in small groups to discuss, revise, and edit their narratives before publishing (sharing) them.

5. Direct students to publish (share) their narratives with either one partner or with the class. They may also share their narratives with other audiences, such as families or community groups. They may even record the narratives on audiotape for sharing at a later time.

SkyLight Training and Publishing Inc.

**Metacognitive Discussion**

1. What are my new goals as a thinker and writer of narratives?

2. What did I do that improved the quality of my thinking and writing?

**Closure**

Lead students to assess their own narratives using the following criteria drawn from the assessment rubrics for writing and thinking about narratives:

a. Was my meaning clear?

b. Was my narrative well-structured?

c. How well did I do with spelling and punctuation?

d. How confident am I about writing narratives?

Likewise, lead students to assess their use of narrative thinking using the following questions:

a. What effect did drawing pictures, adding signal words, and preparing summary captions have on my writing?

b. What effect did using the critical thinking frame have on my writing?

Ask students to discuss the following additional questions:

1. What effect did the narrative writing frame have on your writing? Would you like to continue using it?

2. Can you identify the characteristics of a narrative?

3. Did you enjoy writing about events?

4. Do you have any new writing goals?

Finally use the narrative writing assessment rubric to record students' progress with this form of thinking and writing.

# Catch Them
# Thinking and Writing
# Procedures

# Overview of Thinking and Writing Procedures

## Procedures are

Event-ordered

Sequenced

In the present tense

Generalized

## Writing procedures means using

Procedure Writing Frames

## Thinking procedures means using

Flow Chart Frames

## Procedure thinking involves

Sequencing

Recalling

Composing bias

Questioning

Evaluating

Identifying patterns over time

Identifying cause-and-effect

Inferencing

Generalizing

Linking

## Types of procedures include

General

Commands

Instructions

Operations

Constructions

*Figure Part 2.1*

SkyLight Training and Publishing Inc.

# WHAT IS a Procedure?

CHAPTER 4

Procedures tell someone what to do and how to do it. Examples of procedures include recipes, a booklet that tells how to operate a washing machine, a prison guard telling a convict what to do, a coach outlining how to perform a high jump, a manual for putting a toy together, and directions for road rally drivers.

Procedures come in slightly different text types. They include how to operate something, such as a washing machine or a nuclear power plant; how to construct something, such as a bridge or a tale; and commands to do something, such as an invitation to a party or a parent telling a child to clean his or her room . . . now!

There is no pure procedure, and procedures are even found inside other types of writing. For example, when someone is arguing a point of view, that person may outline the steps required to achieve what they are arguing for.

## Why Think and Write Procedures?

Procedures are essential to the operation of society. They cover everything from how to perform complex surgery to bus timetables. It is essential, if we don't wish to keep reinventing knowledge, that students are able to read and write this text type.

## What Does a Procedure Look and Sound Like?

Although procedures serve a range of purposes, their organization makes them easy to spot. Most have a general structure, with each part serving a different purpose, as follows:

1. Goal (e.g., how to make an apple pie)
2. Materials (e.g., ingredients)
3. Method (e.g., steps in making the pie)
4. Comment (optional; e.g., It is easy to make apple pie that stores well.)

Sometimes, procedures are easy to spot (see fig. 4.1) because they use subheadings, diagrams, or photographs (e.g., a picture of an apple pie that looks better than one we could bake). Another characteristic of procedures is sequentially ordered steps, which may be explicitly signaled by such words or phrases as *first, next, then, finally,* or by using numbers or letters. Things in a procedure are generalized. Procedures refer to classes of things, such as apples, rather than a particular apple known to and owned by the writer of a recipe. Procedures also generalize the reader by using directions that look like this: *You* then add the sugar . . . . Because procedures are about doing something, expect to find a lot of verbs, and the use of the present tense—at any time anyone can follow the recipe and it will, hopefully, work.

Another important characteristic of procedures is detail. Procedures include enough detail to do the task completely and accurately. An author who leaves out a step in an apple pie recipe is not going to be popular with the cook when the result is not as advertised.

Not all procedures look or sound like the recipe in figure 4.1, but they do share common conventions. Teachers may like to discuss a range of procedures with students and encourage them to identify the conventions found in all procedures. Again, the conventions of this type of writing may not be entirely obvious to students, but there are numerous examples of this text type that can be used to make the structure explicit.

# How Do We Start Thinking and Writing Procedures?

## What Are Procedure Writing Frames?

Quite simply, a frame is a structure for holding something in a predetermined shape. Procedure writing frames, shown in figures 4.2 through 4.5, provide students with shapes for drafting procedures. Procedures drafted using these frames are likely to be well-structured but may be insensitive to the audience. Audience sensitivity emerges when students revise, edit, conference, and respond to readers. Typically, to introduce procedure text, a teacher will provide a direct experience of a procedure (folding a paper bird, operating an overhead projector, or writing a birthday invitation), and will then model writing a procedure text by jointly constructing a text, based on the experience, with the class.

# How to Make Oyster Soup

## Introduction

Serving oyster soup is a yummy way to begin a special winter meal. Use fresh or thawed frozen oysters for this soup. To get the best flavor, make the soup well before you need it, refrigerate it, then reheat it without boiling just before you serve it.

## Body

Ingredients

For 4 to 6 servings, you will need:

18 oysters

1 or 2 cloves of garlic

a little grated nutmeg

4 tablespoons butter

6 tablespoons flour

4 to 5 cups milk

juice of one lemon or salt and pepper

## Method

First drain the oysters and keep the liquid. Second, cut the fleshy part of the oyster from the beard (the frilly part around the "meaty" eye). Next, crush and add the garlic, then cook the beards in butter with garlic and nutmeg for 3 to 4 minutes without browning. Then, stir in flour and cook 2 minutes longer. Now, stir in the oyster liquid and 1 cup of milk. When thick, add another 2 cups of milk. When the mixture has boiled, chop it up in the food processor, then separate the beards using a sieve. Finally, add the oyster flesh, lemon juice, and extra milk.

## Comment

Don't boil after adding the oyster flesh. Serve with fingers of toast. Don't keep the soup in the refrigerator for more than a day. Eat and enjoy.

*Figure 4.1*

# Operation Procedure Writing Frame

The purpose of this writing frame is to help you record how to operate something such as a sewing machine or a circular saw.

**Title:** How to operate a _____.

**What:** (Describe the thing you will tell how to use.)

**How:** (Steps in how to use it)

**Comment:** (Inform operators about other things that they should know about, such as safety procedures and repair procedures.)

*Figure 4.2*

# Construction Procedure Writing Frame

The purpose of this writing frame is to help you record how to make or construct something.

**Title:** How to construct a _____.

**Goal:** (Say what you what to make)

**Materials:** (Say what you need to make it)

**Steps:** (Say clearly, and in order, how to make it)

*Figure 4.3*

# Command Procedure Writing Frame

The purpose of this frame is to help you write commands or requests, such as birthday invitations or a notice for a delivery person.

**Title:** A command to _____.

**Who:**

**What:** (Goal)

**Where:**

**When:**

**Why:**

*Figure 4.4*

# General Procedure Writing Frame

The title of my procedure is _____.

**Introduction**

Write a paragraph that says what procedure you are going to describe. Say it in a way that invites us to read on.

**Body**

Describe steps in the procedure. Show each step by using 1, 2, 3 or first, second, next, and finally. Each step might begin a new paragraph.

**Comment**

Write a paragraph that lets the reader know something special about the procedure.

*Figure 4.5*

## Assessing and Reflecting on Procedure Writing Frames

To assist teachers and students to monitor and record progress, a procedure writing assessment rubric is provided (fig. 4.6). Teachers and students may use the rubric to record progress on the objectives. This rubric is intended to encourage formative assessment, with progress reflected on a continuum from dependent to independent production of procedure texts. It may be useful, particularly for the teacher, to date observations on the arrows.

## What Are Procedure Thinking Frames?

Procedure thinking frames help students prepare to talk or write procedures. The flow chart frame is designed to do this graphically. Initially, frames are used as teaching frames, that is, teachers and students use them to jointly write a procedure. Later, when used independently by students, frames becomes learning frames.

### What Is the Flow Chart Frame?

The boxes on the following flow chart frame (fig. 4.7) can be used to record, in written and visual form, each step in a procedure. This requires that students first work out the number of steps in the procedure and then draw a sufficient number of boxes. On and below the arrows that separate the boxes, students insert words, such as *after, now,* and *when,* that signal links between paragraphs.

# Assessing Procedure Writing

|  | Dependent | Independent |
|---|---|---|

**Meaning**

Enough information

Clearly expressed

Keeps to topic

Has voice

Achieves purpose

**Structure**

*Construction Procedures*

Goal

Materials

Steps

*Operation Procedures*

What

How

Comment

*Command Procedures*

Who

What

Where

When

Why

Includes other forms of writing in procedure          Yes          No

No longer needs to use procedure writing frames      Yes          No

*Figure 4.6*

*Using the Flow Chart Frame*

Teachers may choose to divide the class into groups sufficient to cover each step in a procedure. This approach requires consensus as to what will be written or drawn in the boxes. This approach is supportive and ensures that expertise is pooled.

The ultimate test of any procedure is that someone else can successfully follow it. Writing a clear, accurate procedure is difficult. Even students experienced with narrative writing, where much is inferred, have difficulty realizing that a reader may not have the same background knowledge of the procedure as they do. Therefore, each step in the procedure must be consumer-tested to see that sufficient information has been provided.

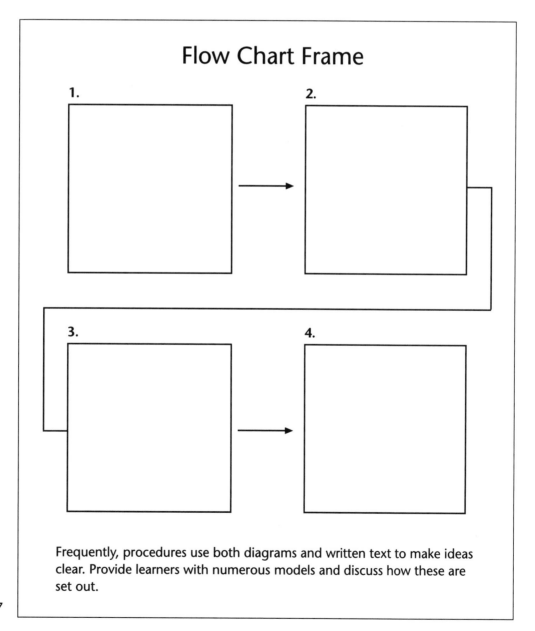

# Flow Chart Frame

**1.** **2.** **3.** **4.**

Frequently, procedures use both diagrams and written text to make ideas clear. Provide learners with numerous models and discuss how these are set out.

*Figure 4.7*

SkyLight Training and Publishing Inc.

Frequently, procedures use both diagrams and written text to make things clear. Provide students with numerous models and discuss how these are structured, for example, how the models use numbers, sub-headings, and comment.

Students might begin by first writing a simple procedure, such as how to put the top on a bottle, but even this is tricky. The teacher might suggest that students first rehearse this simple procedure in pairs, with one student providing the instructions and the other carrying them out to the letter, without any interpretation. Then, they might jointly prepare their written text.

## Assessing and Reflecting on Procedure Thinking Frames

The assessment rubric in figure 4.8 is provided to give teachers and students help in assessing and reflecting on progress in preparing procedures. It is intended to be a formative assessment rubric, showing progress from dependence upon frames and outside help to independence in producing a procedure. Teachers are encouraged to share this rubric with their students, and students are encouraged to use it to measure their own progress.

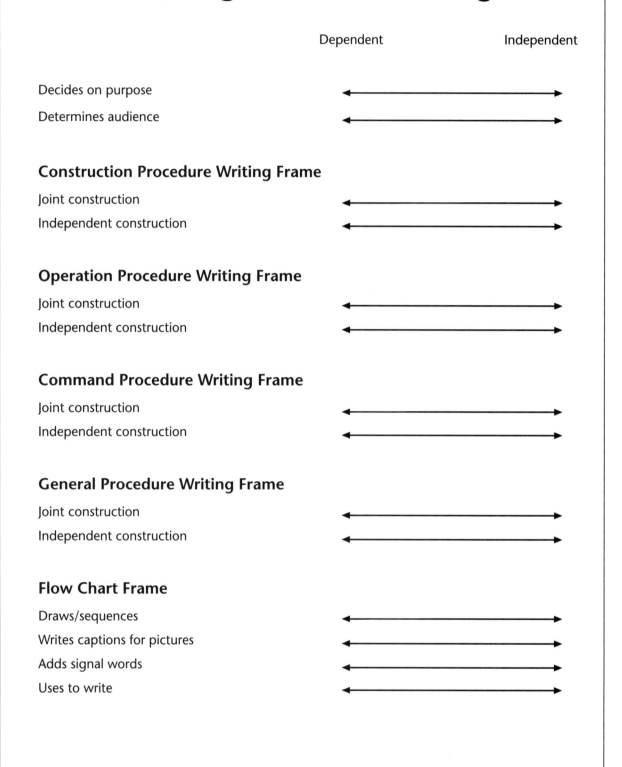

# Assessing Procedure Writing

|  | Dependent | Independent |
|---|---|---|
| Decides on purpose | ←————————————→ |  |
| Determines audience | ←————————————→ |  |

**Construction Procedure Writing Frame**

| Joint construction | ←————————————→ |  |
| Independent construction | ←————————————→ |  |

**Operation Procedure Writing Frame**

| Joint construction | ←————————————→ |  |
| Independent construction | ←————————————→ |  |

**Command Procedure Writing Frame**

| Joint construction | ←————————————→ |  |
| Independent construction | ←————————————→ |  |

**General Procedure Writing Frame**

| Joint construction | ←————————————→ |  |
| Independent construction | ←————————————→ |  |

**Flow Chart Frame**

| Draws/sequences | ←————————————→ |  |
| Writes captions for pictures | ←————————————→ |  |
| Adds signal words | ←————————————→ |  |
| Uses to write | ←————————————→ |  |

*Figure 4.8*

SkyLight Training and Publishing Inc.

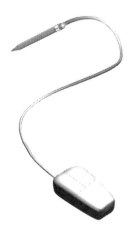

# PRACTICE ACTIVITIES to Support Thinking and Writing Procedures

CHAPTER 5

## Oral Language Activities

**Focus Activity**

# Barrier Games

**Barrier games** involve students giving and receiving instructions. As the name suggests, a barrier is erected between two students (which could simply be the students sitting back-to-back). One student orally relays a procedure to another student, who does exactly what the instructing student says. Barrier games may involve one student telling another the sequence for threading beads on a string, for assembling an arrangement of objects to resemble a duplicate arrangement, or for constructing a shape from building blocks.

### Objective

Students practice composing instructions for a procedure and give and receive immediate feedback on the completeness, accuracy, and usefulness of their instructions.

### Input

To introduce barrier games, teachers might have students sit back-to-back, each with the same size piece of paper and pencil. The game could begin by one student instructing the other to draw a simple geometric shape in a particular position on the paper. Later, these instructions might be written down. Students need to be reminded that their instructions should be clear and concise and that they should be aware of why their partners ask any questions (for elaboration, clarity etc.). The teacher needs to prepare the shapes and paper and distribute these items without the partners seeing them.

## Procedure

1. Ask students to pair up with a friend.

2. Give one student, the speaker, in each pair three cut-out objects assembled on a piece of paper. Give the partner student, the listener, the three cut-out objects and a piece of paper, but unassembled.

3. Tell the speaker to give instructions to the listener so that the listener is able to correctly place the objects on the paper. For this procedure to work, speakers must give clear and full instructions. Listeners may ask questions to clarify the exact position and orientation of the objects.

## Metacognitive Discussion

1. What are successful instructions?

2. What did you learn about giving instructions?

3. Why did partners have to ask questions?

4. Where there any particular words used more than once to begin instructions?

## Closure

Ask students to repeat the exercise. The partners should switch roles and the shapes should be arranged differently and in another position on the paper.

**Focus Activity** # Show-and-Tell

Traditionally, **show-and-tell** has been used as an opportunity for students to describe something. It can also be used as a time when students outline a procedure, such as how to make popcorn.

## Objective

Students practice organizing and wording instructions on how to do something they are familiar with.

## Input

Dedicate a week to show-and-tell procedures. Select five different things that each student could have a procedure for—such as how to build a racing cart (using an example of a go-cart brought to school); how to brush your teeth; how to put your clothes away; how to go from your kitchen to your bedroom; how to feed your pet; or, perhaps, an activity that fits with a current theme of study.

## Procedure

Ask students to nominate a procedure to be shared during show-and-tell time, and choose a day to share. (Note: Some students might like to present their procedures in pairs to support each other, with a third student carrying out the instructions.)

## Metacognitive Discussion

1. What were the successful aspects of the presentation?
2. How might some aspects be improved?

## Closure

Ask students to jointly construct a written text describing the procedure shared during the show-and-tell.

# Visual Language Activities

**Focus Activity**    # Human Sculptures

Forming **human sculptures** is an activity that fosters giving and taking instructions. Sometimes referred to as statue maker, this activity involves one student telling other students how to shape their bodies into a sculpture.

### Objective

This activity enhances both giving of and listening to instructions in the form of a procedure.

### Input

Students need to know that they are to follow instructions to the letter and not second-guess the sculptor. Sculptors need to create an interesting sculpture, but not overtax students' physical capabilities. Finally, all students need to know that, in addition to the fun they will have with this activity, they are to listen to how the instructions are structured and given.

### Procedure

1. Separate students into small groups of three or four. Choose one student in each group to be the sculptor. The remaining members will become either individual sculptures or a group sculpture.

2. Explain that the sculptor will ask students to take certain positions in order to produce a certain arrangement. For example, the sculptor might say, "Stand with your hands straight up above your head and your palms together and fingers pointed. Keep your feet together and look straight ahead." The sculptor directs the next student to join to the first in some way. The result is a sculpture composed of humans.

### Metacognitive Discussion

Students reflect on the quality as well as the final result of the instructions.

### Closure

To check that the group members were paying attention, invite students one at a time to disassemble the sculpture in the reverse order.

# Written Language Activities

**Focus Activity**

# Space-Saving Machine

In creating a **space-saving machine,** students combine several home appliances into one efficient space-saving appliance. They then tell how to assemble the super-appliance, provide a diagram, and tell how to use it in the home.

## Objective

Students will cooperatively draft a design of their machines, then construct a conventional schematic diagram. Students will use the diagram to illustrate how the machine is constructed and to provide operating instructions.

## Input

The teacher needs to draw a simple draft drawing of a machine (such as a machine that brews and pours coffee) and provide models of conventional working drawings. These will often include a schematic of the whole machine as well as a series of diagrams in the form of operating instructions. Providing multiple diagrams means that a group of four students can produce the separate diagrams and talk to each diagram when it comes to sharing the description and operating procedures with the class. Discussion skills might be reviewed, and a time given to achieve the goal.

## Procedure

1. Model a machine and schematics.
2. Form students into groups of four to six.
3. Ask students to design a space-saving appliance. Explain that they are to create a schematic drawing with operating instructions. Give them a deadline for completion.
4. Choose one student from each group to share the drawing and operating instructions with the class.

## Metacognitive Discussion

1. What did you do together that helped achieve your goal?
2. How did the way you talked to the class differ from the way you talk on the playground?

3. What makes a good instructional schematic diagram?

**Closure**

Arrange for students to display their machines and to share them with another class.

**Focus Activity** # Cloze

**Cloze** introduces and gives students practice in filling in appropriate words for organizing a familiar procedure.

---

### Objective

Students gain experience predicting and selecting (evaluating) signal words for procedures.

---

### Input

The teacher selects a procedure with which students are familiar and deletes signal words from a text of the procedure. For example, selected signal words, such as *next* or *then,* are left out of the text. As an alternative, key content words might be omitted. Students need to be familiar with the words that are used to signal movement between steps in a procedure.

---

### Procedure

1. Give each student a copy of the text with word spaces.

2. Ask students to write an appropriate word in each empty space. You might provide a list of possible words, but students should feel free to choose the word they feel best fills the gap.

3. After each student has completed the exercise, review and discuss the appropriateness of suggested choices for each word space.

---

### Metacognitive Discussion

Why did you choose the words you did?

---

### Closure

As an extension and closure, ask students to provide a phrase rather than a single word for the closures. For example, students might replace *Later* with *When the glue has set.*

**Focus Activity** # Critiquing Procedures

In **critiquing procedures**, students review a published procedure and assess critically whether the instructions are clear enough to follow.

### Objective

Students identify and recognize procedures' qualities that foster usefulness to the reader.

### Input

Students should be familiar with the elements of the model flow chart frame before attempting this exercise. The teacher collects procedures from newspapers, brochures, pamphlets, instruction booklets (for objects to be constructed), or from how-to books. The teacher may need to enlarge the procedures to make them easier to read and to allow students to write their criticisms and alternatives on the paper.

### Procedure

1. Form groups of three or four members.
2. Give each group a published procedure to review and to assess critically the clarity of the instructions. They might try to draw a flow chart to show the steps. Or, they might try to follow the instructions.
3. Tell students to revise unclear instructions or, at least, identify what elements are missing from the instructions.
4. Direct students to share their assessments with at least one other group.
5. Encourage students to write to the manufacturer for clarification on any instructions they do not understand.

### Metacognitive Discussion

Lead students to make up a Qualities of a Good Instruction checklist.

### Closure

Acting as a scribe, lead the class to jointly write an introduction to a letter that includes a revised set of instructions for one product. Send the letter to the manufacturer for comment.

**Focus Activity** # Procedure Text Reconstruction

In **procedure text reconstruction**, students recreate a procedure from its disassembled pieces.

## Objective

Students will be able to identify the sequence of instructions using signal words and the meaning of their text, reconstruct the text, and justify the order of each piece of text.

## Input

The teacher obtains clearly written sets of instructions or directions and cuts them into logical parts. The teacher also cuts apart any diagrams from their captions and includes them in the reconstruction activity.

## Procedure

1. Allow students to work individually, in pairs, or in groups of three or four.
2. Give each student or group a jumbled set of a cut-up procedure and ask them to put the procedure back together.
3. Tell students to share their reconstruction with at least one other student, pointing out the clues they used to figure out the order of the pieces.

## Metacognitive Discussion

1. What clues in the text and from your prior knowledge of the topic did you use to reconstruct the text?
2. What did you learn about a well-written procedure?

## Closure

Ask groups to exchange text pieces and to attempt a second reconstruction of the text.

**Focus Activity** | # Inventing a Game

**Inventing a game** gives students practice developing, communicating, and teaching procedures for a game that is initially unknown to its players.

### Objective

Procedures are a key component of physical education and sports programs. This activity requires students to design a game and then to devise and communicate rules for playing it.

### Input

The teacher models a simple set of instructions for a physical education activity, such as jumping jacks. Students discuss the type of language and the design of any graphic that accompanies the text.

### Procedures

1. Arrange students in groups of even numbers, such as four or six.

2. Challenge each group to make up a simple game that can be played by four or six people. (You might choose to design a similar activity around an art or craft procedure.)

3. Ask group members to collaborate as they outline and write down the rules and procedures for their game.

4. Tell each group to meet with one other group. Explain that one design group, called the coaches, will give their game to a different group, called the players. The players will play the game in accordance with the written directions from the coaches, while the coaches watch.

5. Encourage the players and coaches to review the game. The coaches should pay particular attention to the successes and failures of the instructions as reported by the players.

6. Instruct the players and coaches to reverse roles, with the players now giving the coaches the game they invented. Repeat steps four and five.

### Metacognitive Discussion

1. Do you need to change your instructions?

2. What were the similarities between your instructions and those modeled by the teacher?

3. Can you label the sections of your instructions (for example, introduction, summary)?

**Closure**

Challenge the class to select one set of instructions to try with another class or to publish.

**Focus Activity**    # Student Handbook

In this activity, students prepare a **student handbook** that provides procedures to help a new student meet school requirements.

---

**Objective**

Students practice preparing procedures that describe familiar activities.

---

**Input**

Schools may challenge students to write procedures about school activities for fellow students for whom English is a second language. The procedures might be how to order lunch, how to apply for a pass to go outside the school, or how to do other activities of daily school importance. These procedures might be written in English, or in the student's first language, if other students competent in that language are available and know the procedure in question. Students and the teacher need to make up a short list of procedures, determine the abilities of the intended audience, and discuss the qualities of the text and format that might be best for their audience.

---

**Procedure**

1. Arrange students in groups of four.
2. Allow each group to select a procedure and jointly compose a text, writing it on a transparency.
3. Challenge group members to test their procedure on another group.
4. Ask groups to share their procedures with the whole class and encourage students to make comment.

---

**Metacognitive Discussion**

How did the audience evaluate what you wrote and how you wrote it?

---

**Closure**

Send the procedures to the English-as-a-second language teacher or to a teacher with a new foreign exchange student or with non-English-speaking students for a test run.

# WRITING Procedures

CHAPTER 6

## Introduction to the Procedure Writing Model Program

A unit of study about the Indonesian art of batik making for Grades 3 and 4 is used as the model program context. It is a social studies unit on the art of batik making, a technique for hand-applied color dye on fabric. Both flow chart frames and construction writing frames are used. The types of thinking that are developed are sequencing, recalling, composing bias, identifying patterns over time, composing cause and effect, inferring, generalizing, and linking. The specific objectives of the program follow.

The oral language objectives are to help students

1.  explain why steps in batik making are in a particular order;
2.  recall the steps in batik making;
3.  comment on the advantages of different batik-making procedures;
4.  talk clearly to small groups about batik-making experiences;
5.  use a flow chart frame to help organize a speech about batik making.

The exploring language objectives are to help students

1.  explore the language choices made by the authors;
2.  identify the common conventions of a procedure, including the use of the present tense;
3.  use construction, operation, or general procedure writing frames to jointly and independently construct procedures.

The procedure thinking objective is to help students construct a flow chart frame prior to writing.

Teachers need some preparation for this unit. They need to be confident with a simple batik procedure, have equipment, and be in touch with a person who produces batik. To prepare for this unit, teachers need to

1. provide the students with information about batik making by arranging either to view a video about batik making, or to have a batik artist visit the school and demonstrate the technique;

2. borrow a video camera to record the visiting batik artist; but first, ask the artist for permission to record the event;

3. prepare paper, paints, or crayons for pictures and written texts to be produced after session 1;

4. cut out large paper arrows for later use between the pictures;

5. photocopy a model procedure on a transparency for display to the class;

6. photocopy procedure writing frames.

The focus activities that follow are designed as a set of linked sessions to be presented over a period of time. As a reminder that an activity might depend on an earlier activity, the focus activities are given session sequence numbers. Linkage is particularly strong in those sections on working with writing and thinking frames. Earlier activities are not as tightly linked.

# Building Knowledge of the Topic

**Focus Activity** ## The Visit

The **visit** gives students the experience to be written about. (Session 1)

**Objective**

Students build knowledge about batik making and about how to develop procedures.

**Input**

The teacher needs to have explained to the artist that his or her simple demonstration should focus on procedure, rather than on a description and explanation of designs. If a video is used, students should be asked to focus on procedure before viewing. (Note: If a video about or an artist skilled in batik making is not available, the teacher might demonstrate a variant artform such as crayon-dye resist.)

**Procedure**

1. Play the video for the class or invite the artist to provide a demonstration.

2. Explain to students that they are to do the following during the video or demonstration:

   a. Observe and discuss the steps in batik making. They should be able to

   (1) name the equipment used in the production of batik,

   (2) explain the processes occurring in the production of batik at each stage,

   (3) identify the sights, sounds, and smell that accompany the batik process,

   (4) articulate the language patterns typical of procedure texts, noticing the use of words or phrases such as *next, then, as a result, so,* and *finally.* (Remind students of the similarity of these words with the signal words for narrative texts.)

   b. In the case of the direct experience with an artist, ask about safety procedures.

    c. Become involved in some aspect of batik making. This may involve mixing dyes, preparing cloth, applying wax, and so forth.

## Metacognitive Discussion

To what extent is a set of procedures inadequate, compared to seeing the procedure performed by an artist?

## Closure

Provide students with a brief set of instructions for making batik and ask them to suggest additions to those instructions.

**Focus Activity** # Verbal Rehearsal

**Verbal rehearsal** of the shared experience gives students the opportunity to revisit the event and to sort out the sequence of steps. Teachers collect and combine students' initial responses so that the length and quality of what they say is extended. (Session 2)

---

### Objective

The students will be able redraft their initial responses to add content and clarity.

---

### Input

Students need to have been introduced to the process of batik making or crayon-dye resist. The teacher needs all the equipment required.

---

### Procedure

1. Ask the class to describe the part of the batik-making process they liked best. Encourage students to elaborate and clarify what they say.

2. Challenge students to suggest a title for each part of the process such as Pouring the Hot Wax. Record titles in the order of the batik-making process.

---

### Metacognitive Discussion

How did the way we first stated each step change when we thought about it again?

---

### Closure

Remind students that an important discussion skill is helping each other elaborate and clarify meaning.

**Focus Activity**  Movement

In the **movement** activity, students have the chance to re-enact some of the events they saw. (Session 3)

**Objective**

This activity helps students to recall, practice, and organize the actions that produce batik or crayon-dye resist.

**Input**

The class needs to have seen batik making or crayon-dye resist in action.

**Procedure**

1. Lead the class to discuss selected aspects of the batik-making or crayon-dye resist process, perhaps those corresponding to the major aspects identified after the demonstration.

2. Ask the class to act out the procedures.

**Metacognitive Discussion**

What aspects of the procedure did we act out but not talk about?

**Closure**

Direct students to mime a part of the procedure while others try to guess what it is.

**Focus Activity**   Art

In the **art** activity, students have a direct experience with batik-making or crayon-dye resist, following procedures, and using procedure language orally. (Session 4)

**Objective**

Students accurately follow a procedure.

**Input**

The teacher needs to prepare instructions for a batik-making or crayon-dye resist process (not exactly the same as the demonstrations). Also needed are dye, wax, and cloth, or paper and crayons.

**Procedure**

Students follow the instructions to produce their own batik or crayon-dye resist.

**Metacognitive Discussion**

1. How useful were the instructions?
2. What have you learned about writing instructions?
3. Could they be improved?

**Closure**

Encourage students to share their artwork with other students and parents.

**Focus Activity**

# Sketching

In **sketching**, students draw one event in the batik-making or in the crayon-dye resist process. (Session 5)

**Objective**

Students recall the sequence of batik-making or crayon-dye resist steps and rehearse the procedure prior to writing.

**Input**

The students need to have completed a batik-making or crayon-dye resist project or have been introduced to the process via video or demonstration. The teacher should provide materials required for drawing, such as paper, pencils, crayons, or paints.

**Procedure**

1. Ask each student to select a particular part of the batik-making or crayon-dye resist process to draw.

2. Direct students to share their drawings with another student and describe the steps in the process they drew. Ask students to tell which step this particular process represents in the whole process of making batik, what prerequisite steps or materials are needed before beginning this step, and what steps follow and depend on this step.

**Metacognitive Discussion**

Ask students to think how the picture might help them in organizing an instruction or procedure for the event and how sketching might help them prior to writing a procedure.

**Closure**

Discuss this question with the class: What did your partner draw that was not in the written instructions?

SkyLight Training and Publishing Inc.

# Modeling Procedures

**Focus Activity** Modeling Procedure Writing

**Modeling procedure writing** provides students with a look at a written construction procedure. (Session 6)

---

**Objective**

Students will identify the conventions of a written procedure.

---

**Input**

The teacher prepares a model construction procedure for display.

---

**Procedure**

1. Model a written construction procedure, explaining the structure, tense, and use of signal words.

2. Read aloud several construction procedures during the course of the unit.

3. Lead students to use the construction procedure writing frame to construct the goal, materials, and a single step of the method associated with batik-making or crayon-dye resist process.

4. Model the use of signal words and phrases by helping students create signal words and phrases to go with the pictures drawn in session 5.

---

**Metacognitive Discussion**

Could we use a narrative form to write our art procedures?

---

**Closure**

Discuss with the students whether they feel the writing frame might help them.

# Working With Procedure Thinking Frames

 **Focus Activity**  ## Flow Chart

Making a **flow chart** asks students to organize drawings or sketches into a set of sequential steps for the activity. (Session 7)

**Objective**

Students will understand the use of a flow chart thinking frame before writing the procedure.

**Input**

If available, the teacher will use student sketches of the parts of the batik-making or crayon-dye resist process. The teacher needs a model flow chart—either one with pictures only, or one including captions and labels.

**Procedure**

1. Ask students to work as a class to sequentially arrange the individual drawings of parts of the batik-making or crayon-dye resist process to show its steps.

2. Tell students to compose summary captions for each step in the process, using active verbs and appropriate procedure signal words between each drawing.

3. Encourage students to highlight or mark in some manner the words or phrases in the captions that signal the sequence of events.

4. Using the sketches and the captions, lead students to construct a flow chart frame of the batik-making or crayon-dye resist process.

**Metacognitive Discussion**

What effect does a flow chart have on my ideas prior to writing?

**Closure**

Encourage students to comment about how easy or hard it is to create a procedure and to discuss what alternatives might be available at the different parts in the process.

**Focus activity** # Writing a Procedure Together

**Writing a procedure together** asks students, in small groups, to write a procedure for an event in batik making. (Session 8)

## Objective

This activity allows students to practice writing a procedure.

## Input

Students need to be familiar with the procedure to be written.

## Procedure

1. Group students in pairs or in groups of three or four.

2. Lead students to jointly construct a text outlining the sequence of steps involved in the batik-making or crayon-dye resist process.

3. Ask students to share their writing with another group or pair of students, identifying signal words and noting omissions in the steps needed to make batik.

## Metacognitive Discussion

What are the advantages and disadvantages in jointly constructing a written text?

## Closure

Ask students to decide whether they would like to either jointly construct a procedure with the teacher or group, or write independently.

# Working With Procedure Writing Frames

 **Focus Activity** ## Writing a Procedure Independently

In **writing a procedure independently**, students prepare a procedure about the batik-making or crayon-dye resist process on their own. (Session 9)

---

**Objective**

Students practice writing procedures.

---

**Input**

Students choose a part or all of the process of batik making or crayon-dye resist to write about. They need to be familiar with both procedure writing and thinking frames.

---

**Procedure**

1. Ask students to decide on their purpose for writing, such as sharing with parents, caregivers, or another class.

2. Discuss with students that the purpose of writing procedures is to record how to make batik or crayon-dye resist. Explain that students should pay particular attention to the form that will suit a particular audience and that will achieve their purpose in writing the procedure.

3. Challenge students to write their procedures using one of the following methods:

   a. Ask some students to draft on scraps of paper, then talk with you before putting their written text under the drawings now displayed on the wall.

   b. Encourage some students to work in groups under your guidance. Students will jointly construct a draft batik-making procedure, using the signal words and sequencing in the construction procedure writing frame.

   c. Allow more fluent writers to compose their procedures independently.

4. Invite students, either one-on-one with you or in small groups, to confer, revise, and edit their work before publishing it.

SkyLight Training and Publishing Inc.

5. Ask students to read their procedures to a partner, to the class, or to another class or encourage students to make audiotapes of their procedures.

## Metacognitive Discussion

1. Would our writing be different if we had not done the talking and/or actual art process before writing?

2. Will we need to use a procedure construction writing frame next time?

## Closure

Challenge students to assess their own procedure writing using the following criteria drawn from the assessment rubrics for writing and thinking about procedures:

a. Was the meaning clear?

b. Was it well-structured?

c. How well did I do with spelling and punctuation?

d. How confident am I about writing procedures?

Tell students to assess their use of procedure thinking by asking themselves what effect drawing a flow chart frame had on their writing. Lead them to discuss the effect of the procedure writing frame on their writing and whether they would like to continue using it. Ask them to also discuss whether they can identify the characteristics of a procedure, whether they enjoyed the experience of creating a procedure, and whether they have new writing goals.

Use the procedure writing assessment rubric to record students' progress with this type of thinking and writing. Assess both the thinking and writing components of the program. (Note: Procedure thinking and writing assessment rubrics are provided separately [see figs. 4.6 and 4.8]. Summative assessments will be required from time to time; however, the focus in the rubrics is on formative assessment.)

# Catch Them
# Thinking and Writing
# Descriptions

# Overview of Thinking and Writing Descriptions

**Descriptions are**

In the present tense

Topically organized

**Writing descriptions means using**

Description Writing frames

**Thinking descriptions means using**

Character Set Frames

Event Set Frames

Three-Story Frames

FIND Frames

**Description thinking involves**

| Attributing | Brainstorming |
| --- | --- |
| Classifying | Grouping |
| Comparing and contrasting | Questioning |
| Sequencing | Visualizing |
| Observing | Personifying |
| | |
| Substantiating | Linking |
| Justifying | Composing analogies |
| Elaborating | Clarifying |

**Types of descriptions include**

Observation of a specific object or event

Listing of characteristics

*Figure Part 3.1*

SkyLight Training and Publishing Inc.

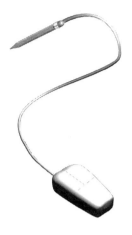

# WHAT IS a Description?

CHAPTER 7

Descriptions are about specific objects and events (see figs. 7.1 and 7.2). For example, they may describe my pet dog Rover, but not dogs in general; they may describe a tornado I experienced, but not all tornadoes.

Descriptions have a number of telltale characteristics, as follows:

- They often include an introduction, which piques the interest of the reader and introduces the description.

- They have a body comprised of topical paragraphs that are organized in a variety of ways and may be linked so that the reader gets a sense of coherence.

- They may finish with a brief conclusion.

- They are usually written in the present tense.

- They can include vivid language and technical vocabulary (e.g., cross-trainer athletic shoes), proper nouns (names and places), and personal pronouns (I, we, they).

- They may include lists, comparisons, analogies, sensory impressions, and reflections about some specific object or event.

## Why Think and Write Descriptions?

When students describe, they are involved in the close examination of their environment and themselves. Description requires a particular way of thinking, a way of seeing the way things are and of working through or coming to terms with the way things are. Description writing is not only a way of recording what a student thinks about some object or event, but it is also a way of thinking, of encouraging students to give

# Model Object Description

## Carla the Cat

**Introduction** (This introduces the topic or subject and the subtopics.)

Because of the curious way she looks and behaves, Mom's cat Carla could not be described as common.

## Body

Topic 1

*Statement:* Carla has short hair, about $3/4$ inches long, with three colors in each hair.

*Elaboration:* These colors are gray, black, and orange.

*Example:* Her fur is patterned like that of a tiger, except that it is all black, rather than striped, around the ears and paws.

Topic 2

*Statement:* Carla has enormous ears in the same colors.

*Elaboration:* They are wide at the base, bell-shaped, and go to a long point at the top.

*Example:* When she is angry, they lay flat down her neck, but most times, they stick straight up like a jack rabbit's ears.

Topic 3

*Statement:* Her favorite pastime is hiding in paper bags.

*Elaboration:* When we unpack the groceries from paper sacks, we drop them on the floor for Carla. She will explore each one, first cautiously poking her nose in, then disappearing from sight.

*Example:* Often we hear a loud purr coming from a bag, but that purr will turn to a yowl when another cat jumps on the bag. Then Carla leaps out of the bag and across the room as if she were flying.

## Concluding Statement

Carla is an unusual cat. We love her tons and she entertains us.

*Figure 7.1*

# Model Event Description

## How Hurricane Val Affected Samoa

**Introduction** (This introduces the topic or subject and the subtopics.)
Pictures of dead and injured people, destroyed homes, and ruined crops remind us of the immediate effects hurricane Val had on the people of the South Pacific. Val also brought disease as the water of Samoa became contaminated; food shortages as crops rotted in the ground; and a loss of income as tourists stayed away from the damaged island.

## Body

*Subheading:* Loss of Life and Injuries

*Statement:* Hurricane Val brought death to Samoa.

*Elaboration:* People died when buildings in Apia collapsed under the force of the wind and the weight of rain. People drowned as rivers flooded through the valleys and as the sea washed over coastal villages.

*Example:* Three fishermen from Pau were drowned as they tried to pull their boats on the beach, and a child was drowned when she slipped into a stream swollen by the rain.

*Subheading:* Loss of Crops

*Statement:* Wind and water whipped up by Val destroyed not only people's lives, but also crops.

*Elaboration:* The wind blew coconuts and bananas off trees, and the flood rotted crops in the ground.

*Example:* Governments from around the world flew food aid into Samoa after hurricane Val because the people had lost their crops.

## Concluding Statement

Hurricanes are a fact of life in Samoa. Unfortunately, Val brought death and destruction. It is a fact of nature that the Samoans will always live with.

*Figure 7.2*

focused attention to their reflections. The topical organization of descriptions also helps students to organize or apply structure to their experiences.

Descriptions are the kind of text we compose after a close, critical, and sensuous observation of objects and events. They are easy to compose, because they are often about specific things that the writer has (usually) experienced. To this extent, descriptions are egotistic.

# What Does a Description Look and Sound Like?

There are several ways the topical information in each paragraph of a description might be organized. For example:

| | |
|---|---|
| **Listing** | John was a intelligent, athletic, and high-spirited boy. |
| **Comparison** | John's table manners reminded you of pigs eating at a trough. The only difference seemed to be that John didn't have four trotters. |

**Statement-Elaboration-Example**

| | |
|---|---|
| Statement | John dresses in raggedy clothes. |
| Elaboration | His clothes are ripped and dirty and rarely see the washing machine or iron. |
| Example | Yesterday, he went to school in a dirty army jacket that looked like it had been run over by a tank. He had to go home and change when other children complained about the smell and appearance. |

The Statement-Elaboration-Example way of organizing information is modeled in figures 7.1 and 7.2.

# How Do We Start Thinking and Writing Descriptions?

## What Are Description Writing Frames?

Figure 7.3 provides a description writing frame that reflects the conventional structure of descriptions. Again, this frame is not designed to usurp the creative energies of writers, but rather to support them.

### How to Introduce the Description Writing Frame

Typically, the writing of a description is preceded by direct and focused observation of some event or object. This might involve students in

# Description Writing Frame

Descriptions depict specific things. For example, the focus of a description would be one dog rather than all dogs. An *object description* might be "My favorite teddy bear." An *event description* might be "My birthday party."

The title of my description might be_____

## Introduction

Say something general about the thing you are describing. Identify for the reader the things you might say about this thing. Make it interesting so that readers will want to continue reading.

_____

_____

_____

_____

_____

## Body

Write your first, second, . . . , paragraphs. Each paragraph should say one thing about the object or event you are describing.

_____

_____

_____

_____

_____

## Concluding Statement

Describe in just a few words the object or event you wrote about.

_____

_____

_____

_____

_____

*Figure 7.3*

SkyLight Training and Publishing Inc.

observational drawing, a lot of talking, and imaging before either joint or independent writing.

The description writing frame should be used initially by the teacher to jointly compose a description with students. During this and subsequent joint constructions, the teacher models the various ways information can be organized within paragraphs, such as statement-elaboration-example, or compare-and-contrast.

## Assessing and Reflecting on Description Writing Frames

To help teachers and students assess their progress, a description writing assessment rubric is provided (fig. 7.4), which also may serve as a self-assessment form for students.

## What Are Description Thinking Frames?

The following frames are designed to help students think and write descriptions.

1. The character set frame is used to describe the appearance and behavior of fictional, historical and contemporary people or animals.

2. The event set frame is used to describe an event.

3. The Three-Story Frame (Fogarty and Bellance 1991) helps students to gather, process, and apply information.

4. The FIND frame helps students to visualize objects and events prior to talking, writing, or drawing them.

### What Is the Character Set Frame?

This frame assists students to describe the appearance and behavior of fictional, historical, and contemporary people or animals. These are all referred to as characters. Students first draw their character (see fig. 7.5), then surround the drawing with sets of words or sentences, preferably verbs, nouns, adjectives, or adverbs, together with summary sentences in the outer set.

### What Is the Event Set Frame?

This frame assists students to describe an event. To this extent it is similar to a narrative, except the event description does not have to be chronological. Rather, it might focus on the description of specific objects or people or actions that form part of the event. To use the event set frame, students first draw what it is they specifically wish to describe about the event (see fig. 7.6), then surround the drawing with sets of single words or sentences, using verbs, nouns, adjectives, and adverbs, together with a summary sentence in the outer set.

# Assessing Description Writing

|  | Dependent | Independent |
|---|---|---|

**Description Writing**

Introduction ←————————————→

Engages audience ←————————————→

Points to content ←————————————→

**Body**

Topical paragraphs ←————————————→

Uses appropriate tense ←————————————→

Links sections ←————————————→

**Paragraph Organization**

Listing ←————————————→

Comparison ←————————————→

Analogy ←————————————→

Statement-Elaboration-Example ←————————————→

**Concluding Statement** ←————————————→

**Meaning**

Enough information ←————————————→

Clearly expressed ←————————————→

Keeps to topic ←————————————→

Achieves purpose ←————————————→

Uses technical language appropriately ←————————————→

Includes other genre in description        Yes        No

No longer need description writing frame        Yes        No

*Figure 7.4*

SkyLight Training and Publishing Inc.

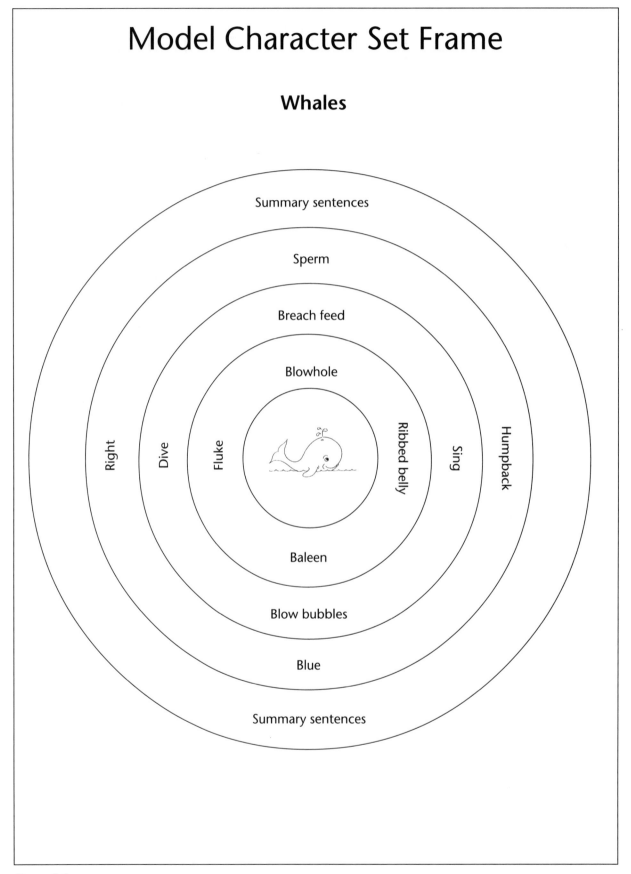

# Model Character Set Frame

## Whales

Summary sentences

Sperm

Breach feed

Blowhole

Right Dive Fluke Ribbed belly Sing Humpback

Baleen

Blow bubbles

Blue

Summary sentences

*Figure 7.5*

SkyLight Training and Publishing Inc.

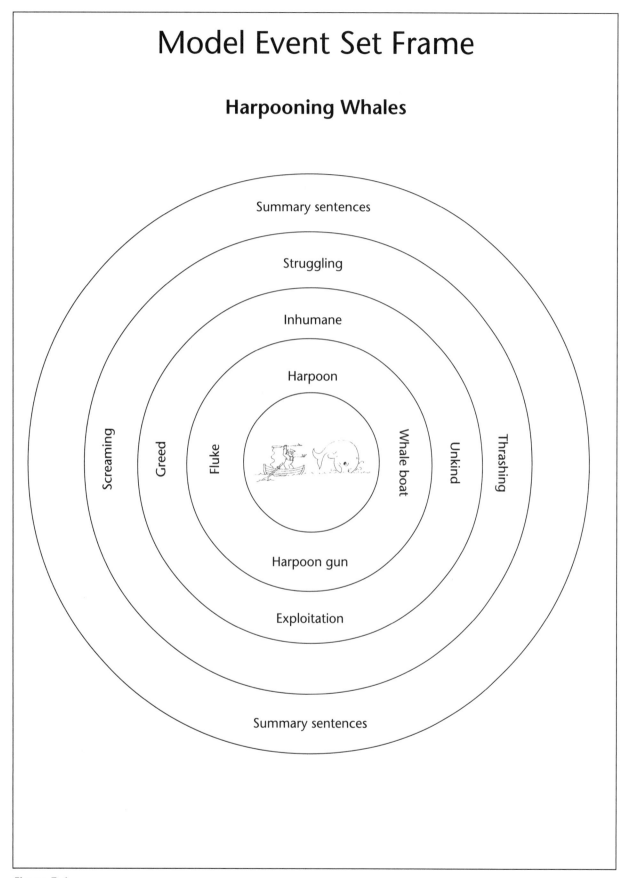

# Model Event Set Frame

## Harpooning Whales

Summary sentences

Struggling

Inhumane

Harpoon

Screaming

Greed

Fluke

Whale boat

Unkind

Thrashing

Harpoon gun

Exploitation

Summary sentences

*Figure 7.6*

## Using the Character and Event Set Frames

### Character Set Frames

Begin modeling the character set frame by reading a short folktale from a picture book, such as *The Three Billy Goats Gruff*. Have students draw one of the characters; then, select one drawing for the rest of the demonstration. Place the drawing on the white board or large sheet of newsprint paper for the whole class to see. Elicit words to complete each set in the frame.

1. Elicit nouns by asking a question, such as Who can tell me things they can see in the drawing? List these words in a first set. Be prepared to write down single words (i.e., if it was the troll, a student might share the word *wart*). Students may even suggest adjectives and nouns, for example, *pustule warts,* even thought the aim of the first set is to record nouns, noun phrases, noun clauses, or simple sentences.

2. Proceed with other questions, including

   a. What do you see happening in the drawing? (verbs)

   b. How are things are happening in the drawing? (adverbs)

   c. What does the troll remind you of? (analogies)

Questions do not have to be directed at eliciting certain parts of speech. For example, two questions you might ask are How do you think the troll is feeling? and Should the troll be doing this?

### Event Set Frames

Proceed with event set frames in a similar manner. There is also an opportunity with these frames to ask questions, such as What happened just before what we see in this drawing? and What might happen next?

Finally, encourage students to use the character and event set frames when composing their written descriptions. The drawings may even find a place in their published writing.

## What Is the Three-Story Frame?

Like the Three-Story Intellect (see fig. 7.7), each story of the three-story frame prompts different ways of thinking.

- The first story engages students in gathering factual information through sense and memory—information about an object or event.

- The second story engages students in processing information— to analyze the parts of an object or event, to make comparisons and associations with specific objects and events, to infer and reason implications and consequences from their description, and to classify what they are describing as belonging to a larger set of objects or events.

- The third story engages students in applying what they know about an object or event—to argue its worth and to predict and speculate on the basis of their description that specific object and events are good, bad, and so forth.

Three-story frames assist students to think descriptively (see fig. 7.8).

- The first-story intellect, which engages students sense and memory thinking, is represented by the (1) describe task.
- The second-story intellect, which engages students thinking to process information, is represented by the (2) analyze, (3) compare, and (4) associate tasks.
- The third-story intellect, which engages students in applying what they know, is represented by the (5) argue and (6) apply tasks.

Specifically, the three-story frame leads students to think about an object or event in increasing detail and depth. Students are involved in following tasks:

1. Describing: Students use their senses—sight, smell, touch, taste, hearing—to describe an object or event.

2. Analyzing: Students take a closer look at the object or event, to notice what objects are made of and what their parts are.

3. Comparing: Students link the new object or event with something they already know. They may recall an occasion when they saw the same object, or they might develop an analogy. For example, students may ask what objects or events are similar to the new object, or what objects or events are different.

4. Associating: Students think of other things associated with or related to the object or event. For example, a hot dog might be associated with a baseball game even if the description is not primarily about the event. Thus, students can be encouraged to state what the object or event makes them think of.

5. Arguing: Students bring a critical dimension to their descriptions. For example, they may think about whether they are describing a good or a bad object or event.

6. Applying: Students describe what can be done with the object or event. For example, when describing a ball, they might say they can throw it or they might think of other creative applications, such as balancing it on their heads.

# Three-Story Intellect

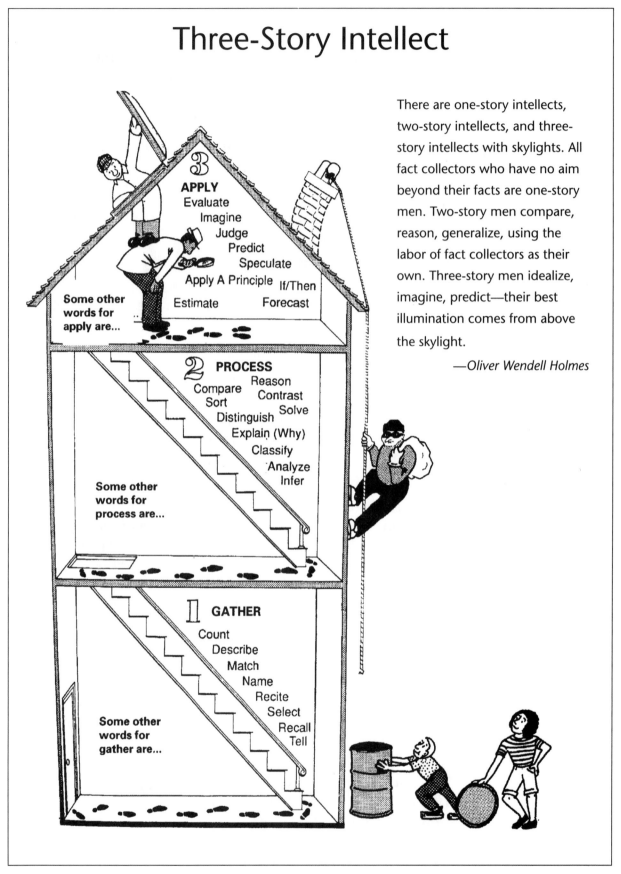

There are one-story intellects, two-story intellects, and three-story intellects with skylights. All fact collectors who have no aim beyond their facts are one-story men. Two-story men compare, reason, generalize, using the labor of fact collectors as their own. Three-story men idealize, imagine, predict—their best illumination comes from above the skylight.

—*Oliver Wendell Holmes*

*Figure 7.7*    Reprinted with permission from *Blueprints for Thinking in the Cooperative Classroom,* R. Fogarty and J. Bellanca, 1991, p. 300.

# The Three-Story Frame

## Describe

How does it look, smell, feel, taste, and sound?

Best sentences _____

_____

## Analyze

What is it made of? What are its parts?

Best sentences _____

_____

## Associate

What does it make you think of?

Best sentences _____

_____

## Compare

What is it similar to?  What is it different from?

Best sentences _____

_____

## Apply

What can you do with it?

Best sentences _____

_____

## Argue

Why is this a good thing? Why is this a bad thing?

Best sentences _____

_____

*Figure 7.8*

*Using the Three-Story Frame*

Use the three-story frame to assist students in researching and writing draft descriptions. It probably pays to begin with the describe part of the frame, taking care that students describe rather than compare. Proceed with the other parts. If you use the three-story frame to help students think about a penguin, the analyze part might prompt them to describe everything from beak to flippers, and the associate part may prompt the recall of the penguin's habitat, food supply, or the use of penguins in advertisements. Ensure that comparisons are made with similar objects, such as a penguin and an albatross, rather than a penguin and an automobile.

The argue part is likely to elicit critical thinking, especially if you encourage students to adopt different points of view. For example, some fishermen may argue that penguins are a nuisance, whereas conservationists argue that they are a good thing.

Encourage students to record words and phrases on the frame and then write their best summary sentences, based on the three (or so) words that they think are the most important pieces of information they have recorded.

## What Is the FIND Frame?

FIND stands for

**F**ind information that will assist you in writing your description.
**I**mage the information in your head.
**N**otice your image—spend time looking at it.
**D**escribe to a partner your image (write, tell, or draw it).

*Using the FIND Frame*

With students in Grades 1 and 2, simply ask them to view closely a simple object, such as a ball.

Next, after removing the ball from sight, ask them to picture it in their heads until it is as clear as they can make it, and notice what is in their image. Then, ask them to orally describe their image (or what they have noticed) of the ball. Show the ball again so that they can evaluate their descriptions. Later, repeat this exercise with a more complex object, such as a leaf, and with written descriptions of objects read to and with the students.

With older students, read a short description from a picture book without revealing the picture. Have students visualize the object or scene, pay attention to what is in the image, and describe their images to a partner. Then, show students the illustration from the book. They might like to share similarities and differences between their images and that of the illustrator.

Note that with events, the image is likely to be moving—dynamic, transforming, or even morphing like in *Terminator* movies. An imagery exercise in this case might require students to sketch a series of pictures describing their images, as well as providing oral descriptions.

## Assessing and Reflecting on Description Thinking Frames

Assessment can be obtained by using the rubric in figure 7.9. Teachers are encouraged to use this rubric for formative assessment, indicating each student's level of independence. Students are also encouraged to use the rubric for self-assessment and reflection on their progress in learning to prepare for writing descriptions.

# Assessing Description Thinking

|  | Dependent | Independent |
|---|---|---|
| **Three-Story Frame** | | |
| Describes | ←—————————————→ | |
| Analyzes | ←—————————————→ | |
| Compares | ←—————————————→ | |
| Associates | ←—————————————→ | |
| Argues | ←—————————————→ | |
| Evaluates | ←—————————————→ | |
| Uses in writing | ←—————————————→ | |
| **Character and Event Set Frames** | | |
| Completes sets | ←—————————————→ | |
| Writes sentences | ←—————————————→ | |
| **FIND Frame** | | |
| Find | ←—————————————→ | |
| Image | ←—————————————→ | |
| Notice | ←—————————————→ | |
| Describe | ←—————————————→ | |
| Uses in writing | ←—————————————→ | |

*Figure 7.9*

# PRACTICE ACTIVITIES
# to Support Thinking and
# Writing Descriptions

CHAPTER 8

## Oral Language Activities

**Focus Activity**

# Challenge

**Challenge** asks students to describe an object or person. They do this by creating descriptors about that object or person and placing them on a grid under the name of the object or person. Students justify to other members of their group why they chose a particular descriptor for a character or object. Figure 8.1 illustrates a challenge grid with words placed by students to best describe the four characters from a story, together with a descriptive sentence about one of the characters. Notice how the students have compared one character with another and used words placed under the characters.

### Objective

This activity helps students to think critically about people, objects, and events. Often it is used to help them describe the personality characteristics of fictional and historical characters, as in figures 8.1 and 8.2. Challenge is designed to help them recall and process information as they read, listen, or watch.

### Input

The activity works best when the number of characters, objects, or events is limited to about four. This ensures a manageable task; that is, the students are not describing and comparing too many things. Multiple copies of a text are required so that students can consult the book as they play challenge.

## Model Challenge Grid 1

| Jane | King |
|------|------|
| determined | arrogant |
| courageous | self-centered |
| sympathetic | proud |
| skillful | worried |
| feminist | grateful |

| Dragon | Jester |
|--------|--------|
| lonely | small |
| fiercesome | secretive |
| unloved | sensitive |
| huge | dreamer |
| sexist | winner |

**The Dragon**

The dragon was unloved until Jane came along. He didn't really want to steal the Prince, because, like the Jester, he was sensitive.

*Figure 8.1*   Based on *Jane and the Dragon,* M. Baynton, 1988.

## Model Challenge Grid 2

| Peiter's cat, Chloe | Karen's cat, Fluffy |
|---------------------|---------------------|
| young | longhaired |
| shorthaired | gray |
| green eyes | gold eyes |
| scratchy | lazy |
| chocolate color | friendly |

| David's cat, Carla | Lucy's cat, Tigger |
|--------------------|--------------------|
| fat | cream |
| dribbly | pure breed |
| poppy eyes | show winner |
| slow mover | bites |
| dirty | skinny |

**Classy Cats**

Peiter and Lucy's cats are unfriendly but look beautiful with their one-color fur. Karen and David's cats are slow and lazy, perhaps because they are old cats.

*Figure 8.2*   Based on a survey of students.

SkyLight Training and Publishing Inc.

Students also need small cards on which they print words that describe the characters, objects, or events central to the text, one word per card.

## Procedure

1. Select three or four fictional or historical characters from a narrative or a similar number of objects or events from a written description. (Note: The characters might be insects, spiders, or mammals.)

2. Ask students to write words on their cards that describe the characters, events, or objects as you read the text to them or with them.

3. Instruct students to draw a grid on a sheet of paper, leaving one space for each character, object, or event (see figs. 8.1 and 8.2).

4. Explain that students should take turns placing one card at a time against the character, object, or event they feel it best describes and then justify their placement to the rest of the group. Their justification should include referring back to the text. Tell the other participants that they may challenge the placement of a descriptor if they feel it is better placed under another character or if it should be removed entirely from the grid.

5. After all the descriptor cards have been placed on the grid, ask participants to order them for each character, object, or event with the most descriptive at the top ranked progressively to the least descriptive at the bottom.

## Metacognitive Discussion

Prompt students to reflect critically on the way authors describe objects and events, and on their own choice of descriptors when writing. Prompt them to appreciate other students' perspectives.

## Closure

Challenge students to select the best words used to describe a character or event and use the words to write a sentence that describes this character or event. Ask them to share these sentences with other students.

**Focus Activity** # Clarify-Pair-Share

**Clarify-pair-share**, used as a barrier activity, asks students to describe an unseen object to a partner by expanding on a beginning statement.

## Objective

Students practice describing with clarity and with attention to detail.

## Input

The teacher needs to supply students with an object to describe—beginning with simple shapes (attribute blocks) and working up to more complex objects (leaves, insects). The teacher should demonstrate the process of further clarifying statements, for example:

> Teacher: My color is red. What else could I say that would clarify exactly what color it is?
>
> Student A: You could tell us what shade of red.
>
> Student B: You could tell us something that is the same shade of red (like a fire truck).

## Procedure

1. For this activity, direct students to work in pairs, sitting back-to-back with one object each. They are not allowed to see each other's object at this stage.

2. Ask each student to make one general statement about his or her object, such as My leaf has veins.

3. Encourage students to pause and think of something else they could say to their partners that would further clarify their first general statements. These clarifying thoughts are shared with partners.

4. Next, ask students to bring the objects into view and share them. Allow further discussion at this stage prior to students writing a brief description.

## Metacognitive Discussion

The important thing here is for students to reflect on the type of statements that helped them clarify their descriptions. They should then try to incorporate details and analogies (red like a fire truck) into their next clarify-pair-share activity.

## Closure

Ask students to describe their objects to the class.

SkyLight Training and Publishing Inc.

**Focus Activity**  # Keyhole

In the **keyhole** activity, students imagine or actually look through a keyhole-shaped cutout and describe what they can see.

### Objective

Writers tend to describe too much, too superficially. Quality descriptions come from focused attention to an object or event. The keyhole activity is designed to overcome the problem of broad and shallow descriptions.

### Input

The teacher prepares a number of cut-out keyholes from cardboard, perhaps making them different sizes. For lessons in class, teachers might like to provide an object or picture for students to view through their keyhole. Make these large so that only part of the object or picture can be viewed through the keyhole (or place the students close to the object). Students need to be paired and reminded that they will have to listen and recall, in detail, their partners' descriptions.

### Procedure

1. Ask students to work in pairs.

2. Explain that one student in each pair should look at the object or picture through the keyhole. (A piece of cardboard with a keyhole shape cut in the middle and held at arm's length will simulate the keyhole.) Remind the partner to listen for every detail.

2. Ask keyhole holders to describe only what they can see through their stationary keyholes.

3. Have the second student in the pair check the accuracy and detail of the description, pointing out discrepancies between the oral description and the object or picture and complementing his or her partner about clear descriptions.

### Metacognitive Discussion

Students might think about what difference (in terms of the language used) a restricted view made in describing what they were looking at.

### Closure

Ask student volunteers to share their descriptions with the class.

# Visual Language Activities

**Focus Activity**

# Sketch to S-t-r-e-e-e-t-c-h

In **sketch to s-t-r-e-e-e-t-c-h**, the teacher asks students to either sketch a scene that has been read to them, being faithful to the objects and actions in the written text (a summary sketch), or to sketch a scene of what they think comes next (a prediction sketch).

**Objective**

This activity encourages students to

- listen to descriptions and represent what they know
- generate new understanding by representing what they hear in visual form;
- predict events.

This activity promotes discussion, which helps students clarify their meanings. The word *stretch* is included in the name because students understanding of a text is expanded as a result of the activity.

**Input**

The teacher selects a written description that is vivid and creates visual images in the mind of the listener.

**Procedure**

1. Select a short (five to seven minutes) description to the class. Tell the students to listen carefully, because they will be asked to draw a picture about what they hear. Read the introduction and about two paragraphs, then stop reading.

2. Instruct students to sketch a summary of what has been described so far. (Encourage students to sketch in pencil and complete their sketches quickly.)

3. Explain that students are to share their sketches with a partner and use the sketches to point out or recall things mentioned in the description read by the teacher. Partners are to be alert for anything drawn or said that was not actually mentioned in the teacher's text. Partners should mention these extra inferred descriptive details to each other.

4. Continue reading. You might choose to repeat the summary sketch activity or ask the class to complete a prediction sketch that illustrates what will be described next.

5. Ask students to share these sketches with a partner.

## Metacognitive Discussion

This activity should alert students to the fact that drawing what they know about a character, object, or event, before they talk or write about it, extends their understanding and improves the quality of their description. They should also become aware of how much they want a listener or reader to infer about the thing they are describing.

## Closure

Discuss the students' predictions. Some of the predictions will be confirmed as you finish reading the text. Others will not be mentioned in the text. This offers the class a chance to critically discuss whether the author has included enough information and why certain aspects might have been excluded.

**Focus Activity**  # Observational Drawings

**Observational drawings** is an activity that gives students a chance to record in detail an object they have been examining.

## Objective

Writers tend to describe too much, too superficially. Quality descriptions come from close observation of an object or event. The observational drawing activity is designed to overcome the problem of broad, undetailed descriptions.

## Input

Students are provided with an object (leaf, insect), sharp lead pencils, and paper.

## Procedure

1. Allow students two to five minutes to really look at an object (leaf, rock, insect).
2. Ask students to draw it (or part of it) in detail. (Note: This step might cover one class session.)
3. Challenge students to describe the object using any form of writing—poem, description, or song. Encourage focused description and the use of analogies.

## Metacognitive Discussion

1. Would your description have been different if you had not first drawn the object?
2. Do drawn and written descriptions say the same thing? What can you do with drawn descriptions that you can't do with written descriptions?

## Closure

Ask student volunteers to share their drawings and descriptions.

**Focus Activity** # Create a Creature

To **create a creature**, students combine the features and characteristics of two different creatures to design a new one, draw the creature, and describe it to other students.

**Objective**

This cooperative task requires students to describe the features of their creature as it is created, to justify its design, and to describe it clearly to a third person.

**Input**

The teacher should gather pictures of insects and other animals that the students could view with the aim of combining them. Students will also need colored pencils, erasers, and an arrangement of desks that allows small groups of students (two or three) to work together.

**Procedure**

1. Tell students to select two different animals with which they are familiar.

2. Ask them to combine the features of the two animals in a way that will make the creature function well in the wild.

3. Challenge them to draw the new creature (or if appropriate, cut out pictures of the two animals and join them).

4. After students draw the creature, ask them to name it and rehearse what they might say about it. Their descriptions might also state how the creature might function in a particular environment.

**Metacognitive Discussion**

Students should be prompted to reflect on cooperative behaviors that allowed their group to achieve the task of creating an imaginary creature. They should also reflect on how well their description was structured.

**Closure**

Ask students to describe their creature to another group of students who ask questions to clarify as needed. Students should report those questions to their home groups who then reflect on the adequacy of their descriptions.

**Focus Activity**

# Creating a Personal Logo

In **creating a personal logo**, students are asked to draw and describe a logo that expresses the personality or outstanding characteristic of the person or character they are working with.

### Objective

Students need to listen to or read closely about their subject, and to process what they find out in visual form. The objective is also to help students appreciate and represent abstract qualities of their subject (such as courage, compassion) in visual form.

### Input

Teachers need to either provide a quality character description (read aloud from a book), or to talk about a famous person (complete with illustration), or to pair students up with a partner that will be the subject of their logo. Teachers should model their own coat-of-arms and logo (or both) noting the imagery and inscription.

### Procedure

1. Encourage students to either listen to the description as you read it or interview their partner and then design their logos. Remind students that logos often represent the traits or qualities or personality of a person, not only their physical attributes and achievements.

2. Ask students to describe the character to a friend.

### Metacognitive Discussion

1. Is the logo a good representation of the person or character?

2. Does it accentuate something out of proportion to its existence in the person or character?

3. What does it ignore?

4. How might this activity change the way you write future character descriptions?

### Closure

Challenge students to display their logos and ask other students to try and interpret the qualities of the subject represented by the logo.

# Written Language Activities

**Focus Activity** # Writing Topic Sentences

**Writing topic sentences** asks students to write a sentence about a topic and then to create a comparison to accompany the original sentence. They use a comparison box, as shown in figure 8.3, to help them identify appropriate features and collect instances of the features in the characters they are working with. The box serves as the basis for developing the comparison.

## Objective

The aim of this activity is to help students use the words that signal the use of a comparison structure. These include *compared with*, *different from*, *similar to*, and *in contrast*. Sometimes these words are omitted or the word *but* is substituted. For example, My cat Carla has a loud purr, but not as loud as Lucy's cat, Tigger.

## Input

A simple comparison box (see fig. 8.3) will assist students to write paragraphs using comparisons.

## Procedure

1. Provide two similar characters, people, or objects to compare and a blank comparison box.

| Comparison Box | | | | |
|---|---|---|---|---|
| **Cat** | **Color** | **Eyes** | **Ears** | **Tail** |
| Carla | brown | yellow buttons | short and round | stumpy |
| Tigger | black and white | black buttons | floppy and long | pointy |

**Comparison sentence** (employing analogy):
Although Carla and Tigger both have button-like eyes, Carla's are like little yellow headlights whereas Tigger's are like small black holes.

*Figure 8.3*

2. Ask students to identify key aspects of each character, person, or object and to record them as labels across the top of the chart. For example, the key aspects of two cats may be color, ears, and tail (see fig. 8.3).

3. Instruct students to choose descriptors for each of these labels for each character, person, or object and write them on the chart.

4. Challenge students to use the descriptors to write comparison statements that include an appropriate link word, such as *similar.*

## Metacognitive Discussion

Discuss how students could use comparisons in their descriptions and what effect these have on the meaning. Discuss the use of the comparison box as a way of organizing information prior to writing a description.

## Closure

Ask students to share their comparative sentences or paragraphs.

**Focus Activity** # Create a Topic Sentence

Students **create a topic sentence** followed by a list of descriptors about the topic.

## Objective

Demonstrate how to use 1, 2, 3 and (a), (b), (c) to list information.

## Input

This demonstration might use words about characters collected during the challenge activity, or words about objects and events collected when using character and event frames. (Note: The following example describes students' hair. However, you may choose to use words from the challenge activity or the comparison box or the character and event frames.)

## Procedure

1. Ask students to select words about hair (such as blond, brunette, auburn, or gray) that go together and provide a label for them (such as hair color.)

2. Lead students to construct one paragraph per label using the 1, 2, 3 list format. First, students will write a topic sentence for each paragraph that lists the words under each label. For example, 1. Darla's hair is blond.

3. Second, students will write one sentence that clarifies each word listed using an (a), (b), (c) format. For example,

   a. Darla's hair is as blond as the sands of Hawaii.

   b. It sparkles like jewels in the sand.

   c. The sun shines off her hair in a way that reflects her personality. (Note: This sentence links to the label: personality and hair type.)

## Metacognitive Discussion

What are the advantages and disadvantages of using a listing format when writing descriptions?

## Closure

Encourage students to share their descriptions.

**Focus Activity**

# Statement-Elaboration-Example Paragraph

This activity asks students to prepare a **statement-elaboration-example paragraph** that describes a topic by starting with a statement that is followed by an explanation and an example.

## Objective

Demonstrate the use of statement-elaboration-example for paragraph organization.

## Input

Teachers should provide some direct experience for students to use (BMX bike, video clip). Teachers also need a model paragraph that uses the statement-elaboration-example format and a paragraph frame that lists these headings.

## Procedure

1. Discuss the thing to be described. (You may choose to use a keyhole or clarify-pair-share approach).

2. Demonstrate how to use the writing frame which lists the statement-elaboration-example headings under a topic. Remind students that the elaboration portion might include comparison.

3. Ask students to work in pairs to write a description using the frame.

## Metacognitive Discussion

Ask students to discuss the value of a statement-elaboration-example framework.

## Closure

Ask students to suggest a audience-engaging subheading for the paragraph after it has been jointly constructed by the class.

**Focus Activity** # Word Line

In **word line**, students rank adjectives used by an author to describe a person or object and place the words on a line that ranks their usefulness or appropriateness from least useful or appropriate to most useful or appropriate, as shown in figure 8.4.

### Objective

This activity helps students think critically about their and other authors' choices of descriptors. Specifically students are helped to define the meaning of descriptors and to justify their place on a continuum.

### Input

The teacher should provide a shared reading lesson and a large copy of the word line for classroom use.

### Procedure

1. Challenge students to identify adjectives that describe people, objects, or events from the reading.

2. Lead students to think critically about these adjectives and suggest alternatives.

3. Encourage students to rank the alternatives on a word line (see fig. 8.4) and decide whether the author's choice was best.

### Metacognitive Discussion

1. How did the author's choice differ from other words that might have been chosen?

2. Does the choice of one word preclude the use of others?

### Closure

Ask students to display their word lists on the wall.

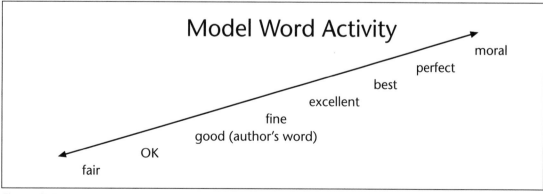

Figure 8.4

**Focus Activity**

# Alternate Titles and Subheadings

In creating **alternate titles and subheadings**, students create a caption for a description.

## Objective

This activity asks students to think critically about the author's choice of title and subheadings.

## Input

Teachers should select a well-structured description, perhaps related to a current topic of study. They should also model how titles and subheadings can capture readers' interest as well as indicate the thing described.

## Procedure

1. Read a description to the class without reading the title.
2. Ask students to choose appropriate titles for the description.
3. Read the text a second time, pausing after each topic. During the pauses, challenge students to suggest a subheading for that section of text. Record the subheadings on the board for later reference.
4. Reveal the author's title and subheadings.

## Metacognitive Discussion

Students might be asked to critically compare their suggested titles and subheadings with those of the author. They might also consider how titles alter one's perspective on the description. For example, if the author is trying to be humorous, would he or she use a different title?

## Closure

Encourage students to come to a consensus about which title and subheads might be used.

**Focus Activity**

# Concept Starter Sentences

**Concept starter sentences** asks students to finish sentences that assist them to write descriptions.

### Objective

This activity shows students five ways to begin describing any character, person, object, or event.

### Input

Teachers need to provide something for the students to describe (such as a rabbit), and prepare starter sentences as modeled below.

### Procedure

1. Ask students to examine an object (such as a rabbit) and compose sentences that begin:

   a. My (<u>object</u>) has . . .

   b. My (<u>object</u>) can . . .

   c. My (<u>object</u>) is . . .

   d. My (<u>object</u>) is a . . .

   e. My (<u>object</u>) is like . . .

2. When the students complete the sentences, point at the following:

   a. Sentence starter (a) helps students describe the parts of the object, which requires a gathering intellect.

   b. Sentence starter (b) helps students describes what the object, which requires a gathering intellect.

   c. Sentence starter (c) helps students analyze the object, which requires a processing intellect.

   d. Sentence starter (d) helps students classify the object, which requires a processing intellect.

   e. Sentence starter (e) helps students compare the object with something else, which requires a processing intellect.

3. Challenge students to expand these starter sentences (which can be treated as topic sentences) into paragraphs.

**Metacognitive Discussion**

Students can be challenged to assess how well the starter sentences would suit the description of people, objects, and events and how they might apply the activity when describing something else.

**Closure**

Challenge students to revise (modify) the five types of starter sentences.

SkyLight Training and Publishing Inc.

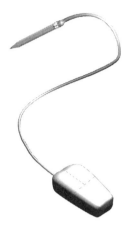

# WRITING Descriptions

CHAPTER 9

## Introduction to the Description Writing Model Program

The following thinking and writing descriptions activities demonstrate how some of the activities described in chapter 8 might be brought together in a program extending over several days.

A unit of study about spiders, aimed at students in Grades 3 to 6, is used as the model program context. It is a language- and literature-based curriculum unit. It includes the use of character set and FIND frames and the challenge activity as thinking strategies. The series of activities stresses the following three types of thinking: attributing—classifying, comparing, contrasting, sequencing, and observing; brainstorming—grouping, questioning, visualizing, and personifying; and critical thinking—substantiating, justifying, linking, composing analogies, clarifying, and elaborating.   The specific achievement objectives follow.

The oral language objectives are to help students

1. organize topically what is to be said or written;

2. use various ways of organizing what they say;

3. listen to speakers and identify how their descriptions are structured and the literary devices they use to make their meaning clear;

4. participate in a challenge activity.

The exploring language objectives are to help students

1. explore the language choices made by the authors of descriptions;

2. identify the common conventions of descriptions, including the use of the present tense and comparison structures;

3. use paragraphs;

4. observe and sketch characterizations;

5. use the appropriate tense when writing;

6. use a description writing frame, first jointly and then independently.

The description thinking objectives are to help students

1. use a character set frame prior to writing a character description;

2. use a FIND frame prior to talking and writing an event description;

3. use the challenge activity prior to talking about and writing a character description.

To prepare for this unit, teachers need to

1. obtain a copy of *Aranea* (Wagner 1989), and *Like Jake and Me* (Jukes 1984);

2. draw character set frames;

3. prepare paper and sharp lead pencils for observational drawings;

4. gather a supply of index cards for the challenge activity;

5. collect spiders;

6. prepare three-story frames for describing the spiders;

7. obtain reference books about common spiders.

Remember that these focus activities, particularly those in the working with thinking and writing frames sections, are linked and are shown with session numbers as a reminder of their linkage.

# Building Knowledge of the Topic

**Focus Activity**   # Tuning In

**Tuning in** introduces the topic of spiders as the teacher reads a description of spiders to the class. (Session 1)

### Objective

Before writing, students build knowledge of the topic.

### Input

The teacher finds a description of spiders to read to the class. Students are seated so they can work in pairs.

### Procedure

1. Ask students to listen and to remember an interesting fact about spiders.

2. Read your favorite description of spiders.

3. Instruct students to first share their interesting fact with a partner. Then request that they share with the class.

### Metacognitive Discussion

Discuss what effect a purpose for listening has on recalling descriptions.

### Closure

Request that students write, on paper strips, single-sentence descriptions based on the book. Display the descriptions on the wall.

**Focus Activity**    # Oral Cloze

An **oral cloze** activity is used while reading a description to a class and allows students to continue creating information to use in their descriptions. (Session 2)

### Objective

Before writing, students develop knowledge of the topic.

### Input

The teacher needs a copy of *Aranea* (Wagner 1989).

### Procedure

1. Introduce *Aranea*.

2. Encourage students to share their experiences with spiders.

3. Use oral cloze while reading *Aranea*. That is, pause, especially before reading descriptive words, and have students suggest what the next word might be.

### Metacognitive Discussion

During the reading, students critically evaluate their suggested words with those used by the author.

### Closure

Request that students write, on paper strips, single-sentence descriptions of *Aranea*. Display these descriptions on the wall.

**Focus Activity** # Finding Descriptive Words

**Finding descriptive words** is a reading activity during which students write (on cards) each descriptive word that is used for a character. The words are used in a challenge activity that asks pairs of students to use the words for the characters. (Session 3)

## Objective

Students practice listening for and identifying words that describe characters and think critically about those words.

## Input

Obtain a copy of *Like Jake and Me* (Jukes 1984). Be prepared to give each student an ample supply of index cards. Students must have previously done the challenge activity.

## Procedure

1. Read *Like Jake and Me* to the class.

2. Instruct students to listen for words that describe each character and to think of other words that might describe the characters.

3. Ask them to record these words on the index cards—one word per card—in preparation for playing the challenge activity at a later time.

4. Prompt the descriptive word collection task by noting words in the text that describe the speech, appearance, and behavior of the characters, as well as suggesting descriptive words not mentioned in the text. That is, prompt students to collect verbs, adverbs, and nouns as well as adjectives.

## Metacognitive Discussion

Students reflect on the categories of description (e.g., speech and appearance). Students reflect as to whether these categories would suit all descriptions.

## Closure

Pair students. Direct one student in each pair to give a word and the other student to decide which character it describes. Then lead students to discuss the appropriateness of the word for the character.

**Focus Activity** # Drawing

Students continue to build knowledge of the topic by **drawing** a picture of a character and arranging the cards with descriptive words (created in the finding descriptive words activity) around the sketch. (Session 4)

## Objective

This activity helps students become familiar with the characters by creating a character set.

## Input

Students should be familiar with the story *Like Jake and Me* and should have a set of descriptive words for each character in the story. Students need to become familiar with character set frames.

## Procedure

1. Ask each student to draw a picture of one of the characters in *Like Jake and Me* and place their descriptive words (as appropriate) in sets around the picture.

2. Review the character set frame introduced during a previous lesson (or introduce it during the session).

3. Encourage students to group their descriptive words (written on index cards) in various ways. For example, they might arrange all the words that describe appearance, actions, or speech in separate piles.

## Metacognitive Discussion

Sometimes authors bias their descriptions by focusing on some qualities of a character and not others. Encourage students to suggest how this might be done by focusing on verbs, adjectives, or adverbs.

## Closure

Invite students to share their completed character set frames.

**Focus Activity** # Spider Challenge

**Spider challenge** is an activity that helps students further develop appropriate descriptive vocabulary. (Session 5).

## Objective

This activity builds additional knowledge of the topic and allows students to justify the selection of descriptive words.

## Input

The class needs to be familiar with the story *Like Jake and Me*. Students need to have a set of descriptive words. If enough copies of the book are available, each group should be provided with a copy.

## Procedure

1. Organize students into groups of four or more, making sure that each character from the book is represented by at least one student in each group. (Thus each group requires four students—one student to represent Alex the boy, Jake the stepfather, Virginia the mother, and the wolf spider.)

2. Review with one group how to play challenge. The procedure for challenge is as follows:

   a. Select three or four characters.

   b. Ask students to write words on their cards that describe the characters as you read the text to them or with them.

   c. Instruct students to draw a grid, writing one name on each space of the grid.

   d. Explain that students should take turns placing one card at a time against the character they feel it best describes, and then justify their placement to the rest of the group. Their justification should include referring back to the text. Tell the other participants that they may challenge the placement of a descriptor if they feel it is better placed under another character or if it should be removed entirely from the grid.

3. Have groups do the challenge activity for one character. (Note: The similarities between Virginia and the wolf spider can lead to lively discussions.)

4. Ask groups to prove their placement of words by referring to the book.

**Metacognitive Discussion**

Students should reflect on how careful they need to be in their choice of character descriptors. Students should understand that focusing on descriptors is one way of critiquing an author.

**Closure**

Encourage students to write a cloze sentence describing one character, placing a list of three descriptors that might complete the cloze below the sentence. Ask pairs to swap sentences and choose the most appropriate cloze word and then discuss their choice with their partner.

# Modeling Descriptions

**Focus Activity**

# Writing and Modeling a Description

By **writing and modeling a description**, the teacher provides students with a good example of what a well-written description looks like. The teacher discusses an animal description with students to show them the form and content of a model description. (Session 6)

### Objective

By the completion of this activity, students should be able to identify the conventions of written descriptions and the options available to them when writing.

### Input

The teacher selects an appropriate descriptive text about an animal. If the description is short enough, the teacher makes an overhead transparency of it. The teacher also photocopies another well-structured description and cuts it into chunks (paragraphs or smaller structural units).

### Procedure

1. Show the descriptive text on the overhead projector and read it to the class.

2. Discuss the text, noting how the text introduction serves to engage and inform the reader, how the paragraphs are topical, and how the text describes a particular animal. Note also the top-level structures (e.g., compare-and-contrast) used in the model text.

2. Provide a cut-up description to students. Ask students, arranged in groups of four, to physically reconstruct the text.

### Metacognitive Discussion

What cues did you use to reconstruct your text?

### Closure

Encourage students to read their reconstructed texts to other groups.

SkyLight Training and Publishing Inc.

# Working With Description Thinking Frames

**Focus Activity**   Modeling Description
                      Thinking Frames

**Modeling description thinking frames** introduces the
description thinking frames to students. (Session 7)

### Objective

Before students begin writing, the teacher demonstrates how
to construct a character set with particular emphasis on using
some selected words to write a focused description.

### Input

The teacher will need an overhead transparency of a character
set or a real example. Students, in groups of about four, will
need large pieces of newsprint paper on which they will construct their sets.

### Procedure

1. Model a character set.

2. Show students how they may select words from each set
   to become the focus of the description. (Select two or
   three of the best words from each set which will become
   paragraphs in the written description.)

3. Help students to jointly construct one or two paragraphs
   based on the selected words.

### Metacognitive Discussion

Students should note that writing a quality description involves gathering words and ideas, comparing them, and
finally, evaluating them for final selection and use in the
description.

### Closure

Ask students working in pairs to select one word to use in
writing a descriptive paragraph.

**Focus Activity**  # Character Set Frame

Using the **character set frame** allows students to practice using the frame to create a character description. (Session 8)

---

**Objective**

Students develop more knowledge of the topic and practice using the character set frame before writing.

---

**Input**

Teachers need the book *Aranea* and large sheets of paper for the students.

---

**Procedure**

1. Help the class complete a character set frame about *Aranea*.

2. Ask students to select one best word from each set.

3. Ask students to write a description of *Aranea*.

---

**Metacognitive Discussion**

How did the character set help you write your description?

---

**Closure**

Encourage students to share their descriptions.

# Working with Description Writing Frames

 **Focus Activity** # Writing a Description Together

In **writing a description together**, students and their teacher jointly construct a descriptive paragraph based on one of the characters from a shared reading about spiders. (Session 9)

---

**Objective**

The class jointly constructs a paragraph in an activity that provides the teacher with a means of assessing students' abilities to write descriptions.

---

**Input**

Students must know the story of *Like Jake and Me*. They need to be familiar with the description writing frame for characters. Teachers must make a mask representing each character.

---

**Procedure**

1. Ask learners to draft and revise a brief description of a character from *Like Jake and Me*.
2. Aid students as needed.

---

**Metacognitive Discussion**

Students complete a self-assessment:

- What do I know about writing descriptions?
- What can I do well when writing descriptions?
- What am I still learning how to do?

---

**Closure**

Encourage students to stand behind a character mask and to read descriptions of their characters.

**Focus Activity** # Real Spiders

In this activity, students examine **real spiders** and draw and describe one of them. (Session 10)

### Objective

Before writing, students build knowledge of spiders.

### Input

A collection of four common harmless spiders and resources that describe the spiders are prepared by the teacher.

### Procedure

1. Share a collection of four common harmless spiders with the class.
2. Challenge students to complete observational drawings of one spider.
3. Tell students to talk about this spider in buzz groups using the three-story frame.
4. Provide resources so that students can research what the experts know about each spider.
5. Ask students, working in pairs, to list descriptors about each spider.
6. Direct students to use the descriptions to play challenge. They should use the names of the spiders at the top of the four grids.

### Metacognitive Discussion

In the previous session, students listed what they were still learning to do. At this point, they might undertake another self-assessment using the same questions.

### Closure

Orient students toward writing independently by having them select one spider to describe.

SkyLight Training and Publishing Inc.

**Focus Activity** # Writing a Description Independently

**Writing a description independently** asks students to prepare a description of a spider or of some event about a spider. (Session 11)

---

**Objective**

Students apply the skills of description writing.

---

**Input**

Students use the outcome of the previous session, together with other thinking and writing resources around the class on description writing, to assist them to write.

---

**Procedure**

1. Ask the class to identify their audience and purpose and to decide who will read their spider descriptions and how they are to deliver these to the intended audience (fax, e-mail, mail, etc.).

2. Lead students to
   a. use the description writing frame to independently write a draft description of a spider;
   b. write one jointly in a group; or
   c. write one with your help.

3. Tell students to independently revise and edit their descriptions.

4. Instruct students to meet with other members of their writing community and with you.

5. Allow students to share their spider descriptions with the intended audience and record reader responses.

---

**Metacognitive Discussion**

Students provide a final self-assessment of their description writing ability. Teachers confer with students and lead them to reflect on the process.

---

**Closure**

Discuss and assess the value of the character set frame and the description writing frame and assess the quality of the spider descriptions with the class. Lead the class to set new goals for description writing.

# Catch Them
# Thinking and Writing
# Reports

In comparison, both should have ta

for three days, after which they

All were used for manufacturing the ste

she wrote two plays while living ir

could be of value if the stock price increased.

during the Civil War to capture the

# Overview of Thinking and Writing Reports

**Reports are**

    True

    In the present tense

    Topically organized

**Writing Reports means using**

    Report Writing Frames

**Thinking reports means using**

    Meaning Frames

    Brainstorm Frames

    Graphic Frames

    Meaning Web Frames

**Report thinking involves**

| Attributing | Brainstorming |
|---|---|
| Classifying | Grouping |
| Comparing and contrasting | Questioning |
| Sequencing | Visualizing |
| Observing | Personifying |
| | |
| Substantiating | Linking |
| Justifying | Composing analogies |
| Elaborating | Clarifying |

**Types of reports include**

    Object

    Event

    Idea

*Figure Part 4.1*

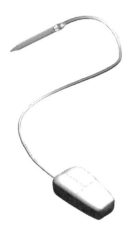

# WHAT IS a Report?

CHAPTER 10

A report is a factual text about a class of things. For example,

- A text about whales, but not my pet whale, is an object report.

- A text about dreaming, but not the dream I had last night, is an event report.

- A text about justice, but not about whether a student's parents should have banned the child from television for a week, is an idea report.

Reports are about a generalized class of things, not a specific object, event, or idea. They come in different types, although they share some common characteristics or conventions. Reports are even found inside other forms of writing. For example, if you were writing a description about your pet cat, you might wish to say something about all cats, which would be in report form. Mixing different types of factual writing (and other sorts of writing) can add to readers' interest.

Although there are object, event, and idea reports that serve a range of purposes, reports are still easy to spot.

- They are often the sort of thing you might find in a textbook or encyclopedia.

- Most often, they are written in the present tense, although a report about dinosaurs uses the past tense.

- Most use subheadings or paragraphs to introduce each new topic. That is why reports are often described as topical.

- Reports are unlikely to include the words *I* or *we*. However, to engage the reader, authors might begin a report with a personalized (first person) statement, such as I love whales; ever since I . . . . Reports are likely to include plenty of verbs. For example, a report about whales might include the words *blow, breech,* and *dive.*

# Why Think and Write Reports?

We do not naturally talk and write reports, at least not when engaged in informal discussion or correspondence. Reports can be somewhat unfriendly. But, reports allow us to record understanding about the world in a way that is impossible with any other genre of factual writing.

Given the characteristics of reports, it is not surprising that this type of talking and writing is less frequently seen in primary grades. A report requires writers to move their thinking from personal and specific things (my cat) to general or generic things (all cats). However, students should never be dissuaded from attempting all types of writing. Grade 1 students can write reports even in single-sentence form.

# What Does a Report Look and Sound Like?

Not all reports look or sound like the whale report in figure 10.1. But they do share similar conventions, some of which are signaled in figure 10.1.

Teachers may like to discuss this report model with students, together with a range of other authentic reports obtained from newspapers, basal readers, and textbooks, and encourage them to identify report conventions and where authors deliberately break these conventions. Some general activities that help students to identify reports are composing a report by writing about an animal they know well or composing a report based on a direct experience, such as a report about the game of baseball after watching a game.

Again, these conventions may not be obvious to students, especially to less able readers and writers. Although it is important that students understand the conventions of a report, these should never be entirely prescriptive. Breaking the conventions, or combining two sets of conventions, can have stunning effects. For example, an argument to ban whaling might have more effect on the reader (and achieve the writer's purpose) if the writer describes how intelligent and sensitive whales are.

Reports are organized topically, often in a series of paragraphs. The topical paragraphs in figure 10.1 use a compare-and-contrast structure, but other structures including problem-solution, and cause-and-effect can be used. These are called top-level structures and help students think in different ways. The paragraphs also use statement-elaboration-example structures, such as those outlined in the chapter on descriptions.

# Model Report

## Whales: Mammals of the Sea

### Introduction and General Classification

Ever marveled at pictures of magnificent whales?

Whales are mammals (warm-blooded creatures) that live in the sea. They belong to the same group of animals as dolphins and porpoises (cetaceans). There are two types of whale, Odontoceti (toothed) and Mysticeti (baleen).

**Body** (Note: In these paragraphs the two types of whales are compared.)

### Subheading (Topic One)

*Appearance*

The mouths of toothed and baleen whales are very different. Sperm whales have huge ivory cone-shaped teeth. In contrast, the giant blue whale has baleen plates instead of teeth. These are like the ridges on the roof of your mouth and feel like your fingernails.

### Subheading (Topic Two)

*Feeding*

Toothed whales dive for their food, but baleen whales feed on the surface. Some toothed whales dive deep in the ocean and feed upon fish and squid living at the bottom. The sperm whale can dive down almost one mile and feed for an hour at that depth.

In contrast, baleen whales eat enormous numbers of small plankton and fish near the surface. The right whale can skim open-mouthed through the water and filter out 3,747 pounds of plankton a day.

*Figure 10.1*

# How Do We Start Thinking and Writing Reports?

## What Are Report Writing Frames?

As we have seen when looking at other types of writing, a frame is a structure for holding something in a predetermined shape. The four report writing frames (figs. 10.2–10.5) gradually introduce students to the complexities of drafting this text type. Again, the frames include subheadings that prompt students to think about the conventions of this type of writing.

### Using Report Writing Frames

Writing frames are used by students unfamiliar with reports. The frames act like coat hooks on which students can hang their ideas. The resulting text is likely to be well-structured, but devoid of authenticity, style, and a writer's voice. These characteristics of good writing tend to emerge when students revise, edit, confer, and act on other students' responses to their writing.

### How to Introduce Report Writing Frames

Typically, reports are written after students have completed a lot of thinking and note taking about their chosen topic. The teacher may then model several reports and demonstrate the particular report writing frame appropriate to the students' needs. But all this begs the question as to how teachers can help students think about information that might be recorded as a report.

## Assessing and Reflecting on Report Writing Frames

The report writing components of the program need to be assessed by teachers and students. To this end, in order that teachers can monitor and record students progress, a report writing assessment rubric (fig. 10.6) is provided.

Summative assessments (the "where is the student right now" type of assessment) will be required from time to time. However, the focus in this rubric is on formative assessment using continuums in the form of arrows. Any assessment placed at the left end of the arrow indicates the student is still dependent on the teacher to achieve this behavior. An assessment placed at the right end indicates the student is consistently independent in achieving this behavior. Teachers may choose to date the arrow when they see examples of specific behaviors. Students are encouraged to use the rubric for their own assessments.

# Basic Report Writing Frame

The title of my report is _____.

## Introduction

Introduce the subject of your report in a way that will make us want to read on.

_____

_____

## General Classification

Write something that tells us what larger group your object, event, or idea belongs to. (For example, dogs are domesticated mammals.)

_____

_____

## Body

*Subheading*
Write a subheading that says what part of your topic you are going to write about (for example, What Dogs Eat).

_____

PARAGRAPH(S)
Write a paragraph that says something about the topic signaled in the subheading. Start with a topic sentence and use the present tense.

_____

_____

*Subheading*
Write a subheading that says what part of your topic you are going to write about (for example, Breeds of Dogs).

_____

PARAGRAPH(S)
Write a paragraph that says something about the topic signaled in the subheading. Start with a topic sentence and use the present tense.

_____

_____

## Summary

Not all reports have summaries, but you might want to restate the introduction or make an interesting comment.

_____

_____

*Figure 10.2*

SkyLight Training and Publishing Inc.

# Model Report Writing Frame

**Modeling Paragraphs That Compare**

The title of my report is _____

## Introduction

Introduce the subject of your report in a way that will make us want to read on.

## General Classification

Write something that tells us what larger group your object, event, or idea belongs to (for example, dogs are domesticated mammals.)

## Body

*Subheading 1*

Write a subheading that says what thing you are going to write about.

PARAGRAPH 1 COMPARES OBJECTS

Sometimes writers like to compare objects. For example, if you were writing about penguins you could say how penguins are similar to and different from seagulls. For example, Penguins are like seagulls because they are both sea birds, but they are different because they have short wings. Write a paragraph that starts with a topic sentence, uses the present tense, and compares the thing you are writing about with something else.

*Subheading 2*

PARAGRAPH 2 COMPARES EVENTS

Sometimes writers like to compare events. For example, if you were writing about penguins, you could say how penguins feed is similar to and different from how seagulls feed. For example, Penguins are like seagulls because they both catch food underwater, but they are also different because seagulls can't swim under water like penguins. Write a paragraph that starts with a topic sentence, uses the present tense, and compares the event you are writing about with something else.

*Subheading 3*

PARAGRAPH 3 COMPARES IDEAS

Sometimes writers like to compare ideas. For example, if you were writing about penguins, you could discuss the idea of conservation by saying how some penguins are endangered and seagulls are not. For example, Some penguins are endangered and should be protected. In contrast, seagulls are numerous and a nuisance and should be culled. Write a paragraph that starts with a topic sentence, uses the present tense, and compares the idea about which you are writing with something else.

*Figure 10.3*

# Model Report Writing Frame

**Modeling Paragraphs That Use a Problem-Solution Pattern**

The title of my report is _____

## General Introduction

Write something that tells us what larger group your object, event, or idea belongs to (for example, dogs are domesticated mammals).

## Body

*Subheading 1*

PARAGRAPH 1 THAT USES A PROBLEM–SOLUTION PATTERN ABOUT OBJECTS

Sometimes when authors write about objects they state a problem, then give a solution. If you were writing about penguins you could say, "Some penguins live in very cold climates and need to protect themselves from the chilling effects of wind and snow. They solve this problem by growing a layer of fat under their skin and by having a kind of antifreeze in their blood." Write a paragraph about an object that starts with a topic sentence, uses the present tense, and uses a problem-solution pattern.

*Subheading 2*

PARAGRAPH 2 THAT USES A PROBLEM-SOLUTION PATTERN ABOUT EVENTS

Sometimes when authors write about events they state a problem, then give a solution. If you were writing about penguins you could say, "Seals like to eat penguins, and this is a problem. But penguins solve this problem by swimming fast." Write a paragraph about an event that starts with a topic sentence, uses the present tense, and uses a problem-solution pattern.

*Subheading 3*

PARAGRAPH 2 THAT USES A PROBLEM-SOLUTION PATTERN ABOUT IDEAS

Sometimes when authors write about ideas they state a problem, then give a solution. If you were writing about penguins you could say, "Some zoos and aquariums want to capture the beautiful but endangered Adele penguins and put them on show. Some conservationists are against this. The solution might be for people to view these penguins in their natural habitat." Write a paragraph about an idea that starts with a topic sentence, uses the present tense, and uses a problem-solution pattern.

*Figure 10.4*

# Model Report Writing Frame

**Modeling Paragraphs That Use a Cause-and-Effect Pattern**

The title of my report is _____

## General Introduction

Write something that tells us what larger group your event or idea belongs to (for example, dogs are domesticated mammals).

## Body

*Subheading 1*

PARAGRAPH 1 THAT USES A CAUSE-AND-EFFECT PATTERN ABOUT EVENTS

Sometimes when authors write about events they state a cause, then give an effect. If you were writing about seals, you could say "Seal meat, fur, and oil were in demand during the 1800s. As a result, seals were hunted and killed in great numbers." Write a paragraph about an event that starts with a topic sentence, uses the present tense, and uses a cause-and-effect pattern.

PARAGRAPH 2 THAT USES A CAUSE-AND-EFFECT PATTERN ABOUT IDEAS

Sometimes when authors write about ideas they state a cause, then give an effect. If you were writing about penguins, you could say, "The idea of conserving seal populations arose, in part, from the use of substitute products for seal oil, and in part from a belief that it was important to protect nature. The effect was a ban on seal hunting and an increase in the numbers of seals." Write a paragraph about an idea that starts with a topic sentence, uses the present tense, and uses a cause-and-effect pattern.

*Figure 10.5*

SkyLight Training and Publishing Inc.

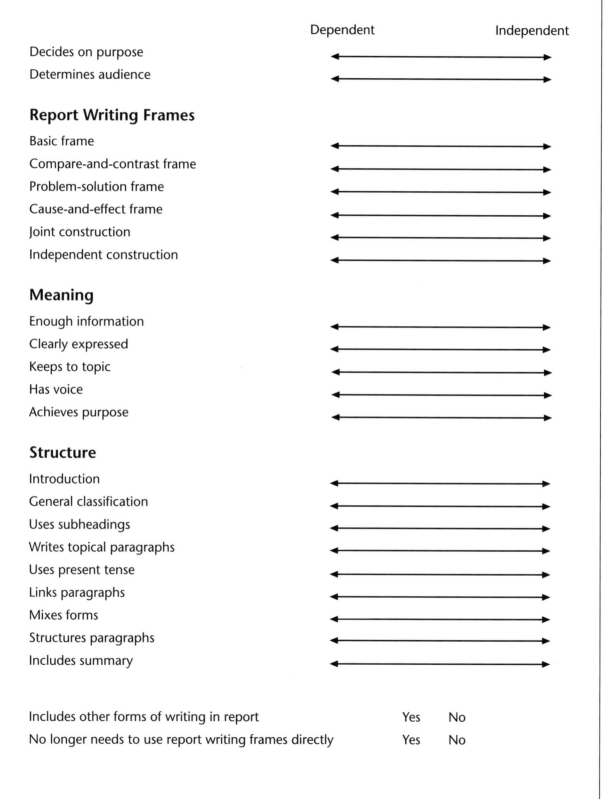

# Assessing Report Writing

|  | Dependent | Independent |
|---|---|---|
| Decides on purpose | ← | → |
| Determines audience | ← | → |

**Report Writing Frames**

| | | |
|---|---|---|
| Basic frame | ← | → |
| Compare-and-contrast frame | ← | → |
| Problem-solution frame | ← | → |
| Cause-and-effect frame | ← | → |
| Joint construction | ← | → |
| Independent construction | ← | → |

**Meaning**

| | | |
|---|---|---|
| Enough information | ← | → |
| Clearly expressed | ← | → |
| Keeps to topic | ← | → |
| Has voice | ← | → |
| Achieves purpose | ← | → |

**Structure**

| | | |
|---|---|---|
| Introduction | ← | → |
| General classification | ← | → |
| Uses subheadings | ← | → |
| Writes topical paragraphs | ← | → |
| Uses present tense | ← | → |
| Links paragraphs | ← | → |
| Mixes forms | ← | → |
| Structures paragraphs | ← | → |
| Includes summary | ← | → |

| | | |
|---|---|---|
| Includes other forms of writing in report | Yes | No |
| No longer needs to use report writing frames directly | Yes | No |

*Figure 10.6*

# What Are Report Thinking Frames?

These frames engage students in report thinking, which contrasts with the kind of thinking required to compose, for example, an argument. The following thinking frames are designed to help students record and manipulate information in clever ways prior to crafting their reports. Initially, these frames might be used for teaching but later they will become learning frames as students use them independently. The following report thinking frames are described:

1. Meaning frame
2. Brainstorm frame
3. Graphic frames
    a. Compare-and-contrast frames
    b. Problem-solution frame
    c. Cause-and-effect frame
    d. Concept list frame
    e. Deductive frame
    f. Inductive frame
4. Meaning Web frame

### What Is a Meaning Frame?

A meaning frame (see fig. 10.7) assists students to research and draft reports. Specifically, it assists students to record, order, and manipulate information.

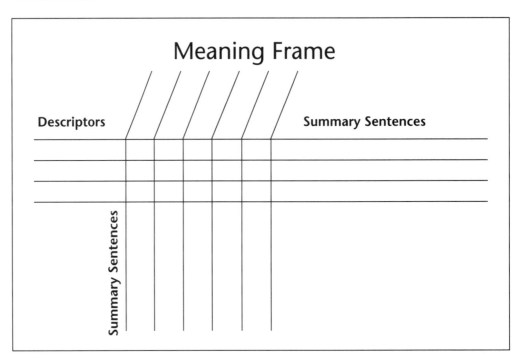

*Figure 10.7*

SkyLight Training and Publishing Inc.

*Types of Entries in Meaning Frames*

As illustrated in figures 10.8 and 10.9, there are two forms of entries that can be used in recording data in the meaning frame grid: one that uses a check, cross, circle, and question mark; and one that uses a numeric scale, such as 1 to 5. The first is more suited to use with factual objects (such as spiders) and events (such as tornadoes). The second is more suited to use with subjective analysis (such as the quality of people and characters).

Also illustrated in figures 10.8 and 10.9 are labels written across the top of the chart. These can be in the form of selected characters, historical figures, objects, or events. Labels are the first thing to be entered on the grid.

All grids require students to construct summary sentences using information in either columns or rows. Summary sentences based on information in the columns can be either in list form, or (more preferably) in the form of comparisons among information in two or more columns. Summary sentences based on information in rows are always in the form of comparisons.

Both grids need to be discussed with and among students. They might try to reach consensus with the numeric scale grid, although this is not essential. The discussion and substantiation that accompany the development of the grids are essential.

## Model Meaning Frame

**Topic:** Whales  **Objects**

**Key:**
✓ = have
X = do not have
? = we don't know or are unsure
O = some do and some don't

| Descriptors | Blue | Sperm | Minke | Summary Sentences |
|---|---|---|---|---|
| Have teeth | X | ✓ | X | Only one of the three species has teeth. |
| Have baleen | ✓ | X | ✓ | |
| Hunted by Japan | X | X | ✓ | Most whales are not hunted by Japan. |

**Summary Sentences**
In contrast to sperm whale
Only Japan hunts Minke

*Figure 10.8*

SkyLight Training and Publishing Inc.

## Model Meaning Frame

**Topic:** Little Red Riding Hood

People

**Key:**
1 = does *not* have a lot of this characteristic

5 = has lots of this characteristic

| Descriptors | Wolf | Little Red Riding Hood | Woodcutter | Grandma | Summary Sentences |
|---|---|---|---|---|---|
| Cunning | 5 | 1 | 4 | 1 | In some ways the wolf and wood cutter were similar. |
| Naive | 1 | 5 | 1 | 4 | Young children and old people are naive. |
| Courageous | 4 | 1 | 5 | 1 | |
| Feeble | 1 | 3 | 1 | 5 | |

**Summary Sentences:** Wolf and Grandma were different. Feeble people might also be naive.

*Figure 10.9*

## What Is a Brainstorm Frame?

This complex brainstorm frame (fig. 10.10) assists students to research, record, and think about information prior to writing reports and to assess learning toward the end of a study.

### Using a Brainstorm Frame

There are five stages in a brainstorm frame (see fig. 10.10). These stages, which should be introduced gradually, follow:

Stage 1. Collecting words

The topic is announced by the teacher. Students list all the words they can think of that relate to the topic (in groups or as a class with the teacher acting as scribe).

Stage 2. Grouping words and labeling groups

The teacher (or group leader) asks, "Can we find two words in our collection that we think go together in some way?" One student nominates a pair of words. This student is then asked, "Why do they go together?" and then "What are they both about?" The answer to the second question provides the label for the two words. Both the label and the pair of words are recorded.

SkyLight Training and Publishing Inc.

# Brainstorm Frame

| Collection | (label) (group) | Questions about words |
| --- | --- | --- |
| | (label) (group) | Questions about labels |
| | (label) (group) | **B.Y.O.Q.** (bring your own questions) |

*Figure 10.10*

Stage 3. Enlarging groups

Students are asked for other words that might be added under the label (these may be from the collection or additional words). Stages 2 and 3 are then repeated.

Stage 4. Questioning the unknown

Students make up questions based on the words that they do not know. For example, in the model in figure 10.11, a student may not know the meaning of the word *spermaceti*. Questions can also be designed around labels. There may be only a few words under some labels, perhaps indicating the students did not know much about this aspect of the topic. Finally, students can ask their own questions and record them under B.Y.O.Q. (bring your own questions). For example, in figure 10.11, one student really wanted to know if Moby Dick was a real whale.

Stage 5. Researching questions

Students suggest where they might find answers to their questions (which may be right then and there from other students in the class).

# Model Brainstorm Frame

| Collection | Species | (label) | Questions about words |
|---|---|---|---|
| fluke | blue | (group) | What is spermaceti? |
| whaleboat | sperm | | |
| scrimshaw | | | |
| baleen | | | |
| blubber | Hunting | (label) | Questions about labels |
| harpoon | harpoon | (group) | What other country hunts whales? |
| blue | Japan | | |
| mammals | breech | | |
| sperm | whaleboat | | |
| blowhole | | | |
| Japan | | | |
| huge | Body | (label) | B.Y.O.Q. (bring your own questions) |
| teeth | fluke | (group) | Was Moby Dick a real whale? |
| callosities | baleen | | |
| swims | blubber | (group) | |
| sounding | blowhole | | |
| migrate | teeth | | |
| breech | callosities | | |
| flipper | | | |
| calves | | | |
| dive | | | |
| spermaceti | | | |

*Figure 10.11*

When the brainstorm frame is complete, the labels can be used as the basis of subheadings for a report, although more appealing subheadings would be welcome. The groups of words under the labels can provide key words (and correct spellings) for the topical paragraphs. The questions can raise possibilities for further research and new sections for the report.

## What Are Graphic Frames?

Information in the paragraphs of a report (and other types of text) is typically organized using one or more of the following top-level structures:

1. compare-and-contrast
2. problem-solution
3. cause-and-effect
4. concept list

Each of these structures leads to its own ways of thinking, such as comparative thinking and problem-solution thinking. Graphic frames help students organize information in paragraphs using these structures.

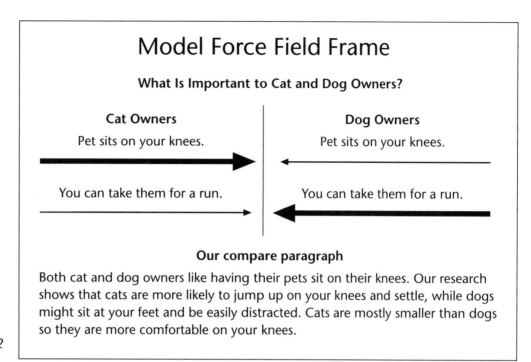

*Figure 10.12*

### Force Field Analysis Frame: A Compare-and-Contrast Frame

This frame helps students compare the relative importance of information. For example, figure 10.12 illustrates how relatively important it is to cat and dog owners that their animals sit on their knees.

Students should first decide what they want to compare, such as what is important to cat owners and what is important to dog owners, and list these. (Note: At this stage they might think of something important to dog owners that they had not considered as important to cat owners). These important things are listed in the force field frame. Finally, students draw arrows under the points listed—the thickness of the arrow indicating the importance of the point. For example, Figure 10.12 suggests that it is important to dog owners that they are able to take their pets for a run, but that this is less important for cat owners. Finally, students can write paragraphs using a compare-and-contrast top-level structure based on information displayed within the force field frame.

### Venn Diagram Frame: Another Compare-and-Contrast Frame

The Venn diagram frame (see fig. 10.13) also helps students compare information. Students first identify the things they want to compare, such as cats and dogs; then, they list the characteristics of each animal on a scrap of paper outside the Venn diagram frame. Next, they identify similarities and differences and determine if the characteristics are shared or held independently. Then, they complete the Venn frame by inserting the characteristics in the appropriate space (only cats, both cats and dogs, only dogs). Students then write paragraphs with a compare-and-contrast structure using the information displayed in the Venn diagram.

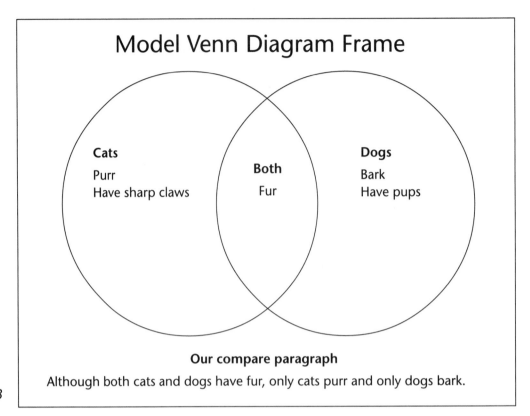

*Figure 10.13*

*Problem-Solution Frame: To Resolve Problems*
The problem-solution frame helps students organize information so they can clearly state a problem and think through the best solutions before draft writing. Students first state the problem, such as There are too many accidents involving bicycles and cars. This is written in The Problem box (see fig. 10.14).

Next, they brainstorm solutions. For example, under Solution 1, they might enter Ban riders under the age of ten from riding bikes. Under Solution 2, they might enter Have special bike lanes on sidewalks and Have cyclists wear day-glow clothing. Students choose the best solution and record it under Our Best Solution. This may be Solution 1, Solution 2, or a combination of both. This solution forms the basis of the students' problem-solution structured paragraph. It might be useful for students to use a PMI chart for each solution: list P (positive) features, M (minus or negative) features, and I (interesting) outcomes. This helps students compare solutions using the same criteria.

*Cause-and-Effect Frame: To Illustrate Processes*
A cause-and-effect frame (see fig. 10.15) has a special place in the factual writing of science and history. (See also chapter 13 for discussion about the importance of cause-and-effect writing and thinking in scientific explanations.) These frames help students see single causes and multiple effects at a glance.

# Problem-Solution Frame

**The Problem**

_____

_____

**Solution 1**

_____

_____

_____

**Solution 2**

_____

_____

_____

**Our Best Solution**

_____

_____

*Figure 10.14*

# Model Cause-and-Effect Frame

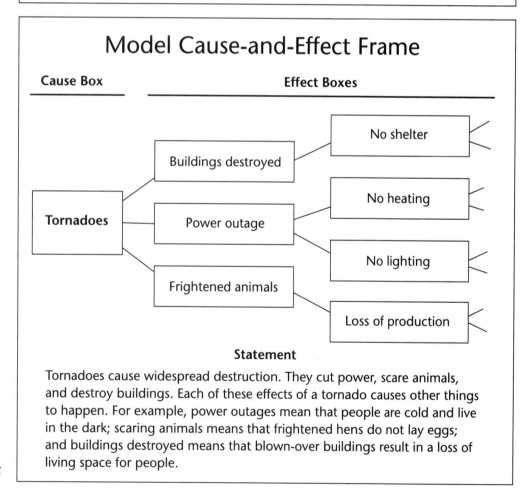

**Cause Box**

**Effect Boxes**

Tornadoes

Buildings destroyed

Power outage

Frightened animals

No shelter

No heating

No lighting

Loss of production

**Statement**

Tornadoes cause widespread destruction. They cut power, scare animals, and destroy buildings. Each of these effects of a tornado causes other things to happen. For example, power outages mean that people are cold and live in the dark; scaring animals means that frightened hens do not lay eggs; and buildings destroyed means that blown-over buildings result in a loss of living space for people.

*Figure 10.15*

To construct a cause-and-effect frame, students first state the cause, such as the advent of a tornado (see fig. 10.15). They then fill in the effect boxes, noting that any one effect may have many secondary effects. For example, one effect of a tornado might be a loss of electric power, but there are many other effects that result from a loss of power, such as a loss of heating. Figure 10.15 also illustrates how a cause-and-effect frame might be used to think about the destruction of buildings and the secondary effects of that destruction—prior to writing such a paragraph. The other effect boxes in the frame can also be used in the same way to construct new paragraphs.

If students were using a report writing frame to write about tornadoes, they might first note what a tornado is, then, at some point in the body of the text, use a cause-and-effect frame to write a paragraph.

### Concept List Frame: For Single Descriptions

A concept list frame (see figs. 10.16 and 10.17) assists students to research, record, and think about information prior to writing reports. Unlike the frames described earlier, students simply use concept frames to describe, in list form, the characteristics of the things that will form the topic of their reports.

There are five parts to an object concept list frame:

1. Can . . . prompts students to list all the things the concept can do. This is the dynamic part of the concept. (For example, a dog *can* bark.)

2. We can . . . prompts students to list all the things we can do with the concept. (For example, *we can* wash the dog.)

3. Examples . . . are simply other examples of the concept. (For example, if the concept were dogs, then Alsatian, English spaniel, and so forth might be listed under examples in this part of the concept frame.)

4. Are . . . (or Is . . . ) prompts students to list the attributes of the concept. (For example, dogs *are* good friends.)

5. Have . . . (or Has . . .) prompts students to list the properties of the concept. (For example, dogs *have* teeth, paws, and so forth.)

Students, preferably in small, mixed ability groups, can use the five different headings provided in a concept list frame to help them think about any object (see fig. 10.16), or event (see fig. 10.17). They can then pool their ideas using a blank concept list frame and select the descriptors listed under each part to help them write the topical sections of their reports.

### What Are Deductive and Inductive Frames?

Other graphic frames can be designed to engage students in either inductive or deductive thinking. In contrast to the frames described above, completing deductive and inductive frames usually results in topic-based some, all, or none statements.

SkyLight Training and Publishing Inc.

## Model Concept List Frame
### Object

**Can . . .**

cut
dissolve
sparkle
refract light
shatter

**We can . . .**

shine them
cut them
mount them
trade them

**Examples are . . .**

diamond
quartz
aquamarine
sugar
salt
jelly crystals

**CRYSTALS (Object)**

**Are . . .**

semi-precious
hard
made under pressure
beautiful

**Have . . .**

facets
value
many uses

*Figure 10.16*

## Model Concept List Frame
### Event

**Can . . .**

help you get fit
be fun
be competitive
save your life

**Examples are . . .**

crawl
breast stroke
backstroke
butterfly

**SWIMMING (Event)**

**Is . . .**

a recreation
a sport
not something we can all do

**Has . . .**

many followers
a place in the Olympics
coaches

*Figure 10.17*

**Deductive Frame**   A deductive frame prompts students to consider a whole concept, such as fruit (see fig. 10.18), and then think about each of its parts. In a report about fruit, the parts become subheadings for the different sections.

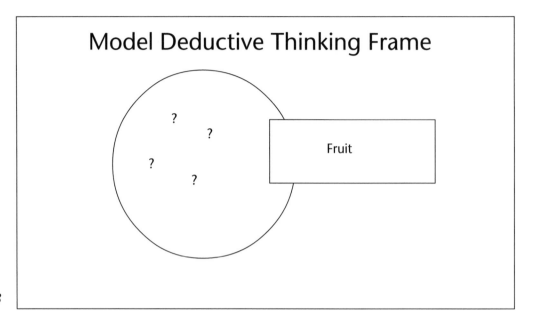

*Figure 10.18*

**Inductive Frame**   An inductive frame (fig. 10.19) asks students to consider the parts and then think of a generalization that describes the whole. There will probably be many alternatives as to what students see as the whole. For example, the whole might be fruit, but equally it could be things eaten by birds!

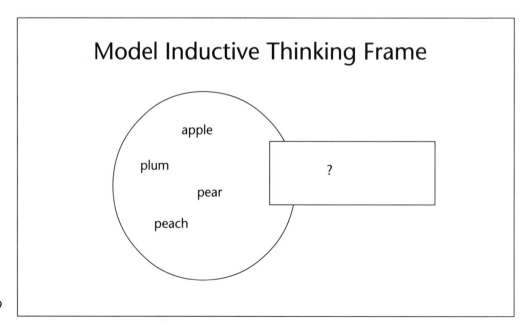

*Figure 10.19*

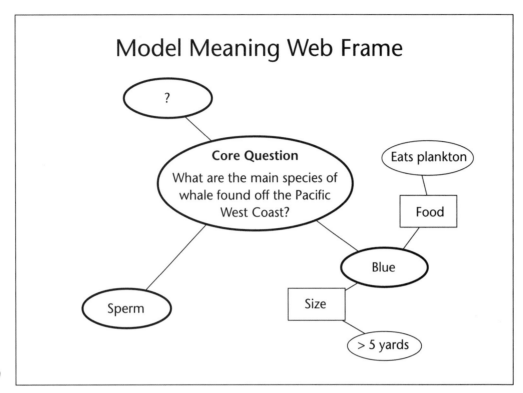

## Model Meaning Web Frame

*Figure 10.20*

## What Is a Meaning Web Frame?

In contrast to other frames, a core question is central to the construction of a meaning web frame (see fig. 10.20). Answers to the core question are linked by means of web strands and support strands. The web strands link the main answers to the core questions. The support strands link details to these main answers.

## Using a Meaning Web Frame

If students were to write a report based on the core question in figure 10.20, the answers in the thick elliptical shapes would form the main topics indicated in the report as subheadings. The support strands, the thin lines and boxes identifying critical features of the main answer, indicate paragraph topics and provide details for each paragraph. When researching a topic, readers can record information in the form of a meaning web. Alternatively, teachers can design incomplete meaning webs to guide students as they read and take notes.

# Assessing and Reflecting on Report Thinking Frames

The assessment rubric for report thinking (fig. 10.21) is intended for formative assessment and uses a continuum ranging from dependent to independent. Teachers and students are encouraged to use the rubric to track progress.

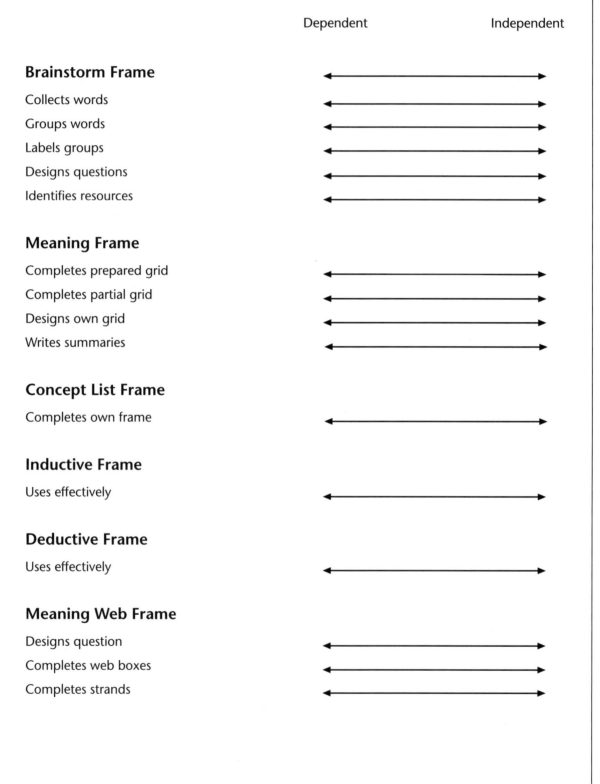

# Assessing Report Thinking

|  | Dependent | Independent |
|---|---|---|
| **Brainstorm Frame** | ← | → |
| Collects words | ← | → |
| Groups words | ← | → |
| Labels groups | ← | → |
| Designs questions | ← | → |
| Identifies resources | ← | → |
| **Meaning Frame** | | |
| Completes prepared grid | ← | → |
| Completes partial grid | ← | → |
| Designs own grid | ← | → |
| Writes summaries | ← | → |
| **Concept List Frame** | | |
| Completes own frame | ← | → |
| **Inductive Frame** | | |
| Uses effectively | ← | → |
| **Deductive Frame** | | |
| Uses effectively | ← | → |
| **Meaning Web Frame** | | |
| Designs question | ← | → |
| Completes web boxes | ← | → |
| Completes strands | ← | → |

*Figure 10.21*

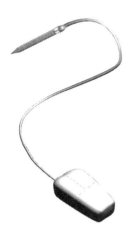

# PRACTICE ACTIVITIES
## to Support Thinking and Writing Reports

CHAPTER 11

## Oral Language Activities

Oral language activities help students further process what they know about the topic and practice using the present tense, typical of report texts.

**Focus Activity**

# Envoy

In **envoy**, each group sends an envoy to a host group. The envoy both reports the outcome of the home group's discussion and returns with a summary of what the host group said.

---

**Objective**

Envoy is a form of classroom organization that encourages listening and that assists students in sharing their ideas with other groups.

---

**Input**

Students need a shared experience to serve as the basis for this activity. This experience might be a reading by the teacher or a shared reading with the class. They are told that there are two groups: their own group, called their home group, and the group they visit, called the host group. The teacher can use the terms *host* and *home* to direct the activity. The envoy activity can be used in all curriculum areas.

**Procedure**

1. Form groups of four or five students.

2. Encourage students to discuss the topic in their home group.

3. Tell groups to choose one member to be the envoy. Ask the envoy to go to the group on their right. Prompt the envoy to tell this host group what his or her home group knows about the topic.

4. Finally, instruct the envoy to listen to what the host group knows about the topic and return to his or her home group to share this information.

**Metacognitive Discussion**

1. What skills, as a group and as individuals, did you need so that envoy was a success?

2. How did this activity assist you to learn more about the topic?

**Closure**

Ask groups to discuss this question: What do we now know that we did know before the envoy activity?

**Focus Activity**　Jigsaw

**Jigsaw** is a group activity in which each student is a member of both a home group and an expert group. After the class or teacher divides the report topic into subtopics, each student in a home group is designated the expert for one of those subtopics. This student works with other designated experts in an expert group to build knowledge about that part of the report. Experts then return to their home groups and share that knowledge with the other home group members.

## Objective

Jigsaw provides a form of organization that encourages listening, reporting, and the specialized research needed prior to writing a report. It also assists students in sharing their research with their home group and with the class.

## Input

Introduce and discuss a curriculum-related report topic. Divide the topic into specific parts. (For example, if the topic is raccoons, the parts could include habitat, feeding, distribution, reproduction, and so forth.) This activity may be completed over several sessions, allowing the experts to meet, research, and develop their knowledge before returning to their home group to share information.

## Procedure

1. Organize home groups and assign a number to each student in a group. The number of members in each group is determined by the number of subtopics to be researched—six is an optimum size. (Note: The subtopics may have come from the labels in a brainstorm frame.)

2. Prompt all students with identical numbers to form expert groups that investigate a specific aspect of the report topic.

3. Tell each group to prepare a summary of what they know about their aspect of the topic. Then ask individuals to return to their home groups to share the summary.

## Metacognitive Discussion

1. What are the advantages and disadvantages of joining an expert group?

2. What questions have the experts left unanswered?

3. What does this activity tell us about how to learn?

**Closure**

Encourage the class to suggest how the expert group information might be shared and to set goals aimed at improving the
use of jigsaw next time.

**Focus Activity** # Response Statements

**Response statements** is an activity that requires teachers to write statements in the present tense and students to respond with an assessment of Agree, Disagree, Not Sure, or Partly Agree.

## Objective

This activity allows the teacher to assess students prior knowledge and students to share and remind themselves of what they do know about a topic.

## Input

Teachers need to construct a list of statements that represent key concepts about a forthcoming topic of study. These are listed as a graph. Students are organized into groups of about four, one taking the role of reporter.

## Procedure

1. Arrange students in discussion groups of three or four members. Designate one student (perhaps the one whose birthday is closest to the activity day) as the reporter.

2. Read statements, one at a time.

3. Allow students to discuss and determine their group response to each statement.

4. Prompt each reporter to give his or her group's response. Record the responses on the board or overhead in a graph (see fig. 11.1).

| Topic: Whales | | | | |
|---|---|---|---|---|
| Statements | Agree | Partly Agree | Disagree | Not Sure |
| Whales are mammals. | ✓✓ | ✓ | ✓✓ | |
| The tail of a whale is called the fluke. | ✓✓ | ✓ | | ✓✓ |
| Blue whales have baleen. | ✓✓✓ | | ✓ | ✓ |

*Figure 11.1*

5. After all the responses have been recorded, to look at the graph and identify where confusions and ignorance are, to set research questions, and to serve as the basis of discussion. (If only one or two groups mark disagree, the other groups might be able to provide clarification.)

**Metacognitive Discussion**

1.  How does this activity help us learn?

2.  How might the graph be used during and after we learn more about this topic?

**Closure**

Revisit the graph, displayed on the bulletin board or wall, during the course of the activity.

SkyLight Training and Publishing Inc.

**Focus Activity** # Completing Statements

**Completing statements** is an activity that asks teachers to write incomplete statements in the present tense and students to complete them.

## Objective

This activity allows the teacher to assess students' prior knowledge and students to share and remind themselves of what they do know about a topic.

## Input

The teacher needs to prepare questions of fact that are relevant to a shared topic for the class. These might be based on the concept list frame. For example, Whales are . . . ; The tail of a whale is . . . ; Blue whales have . . . ; Whales can . . . .

## Procedure

1. Arrange students in small groups of three or four members.
2. Present the beginning of each statement.
3. Encourage groups to discuss each statement and agree to a completed statement.
4. Ask groups to share their statements with the class.
5. Lead the class to discuss the group statements. Encourage students to reach consensus on accuracy and to point out discrepancies.
6. Ask the class to jointly decide on a final completed statement. Record the statement.

## Metacognitive Discussion

1. How does this activity help us learn?
2. How might the graph be used during and after we learn more about this topic?

## Closure

Display the jointly constructed completed statements on the wall and in students' folders or both.

# Visual Language Activities

**Focus Activity**   ## Video Report

In the **video report** activity, students compose their own report script to accompany a video.

---

**Objective**

This activity develops students' knowledge about the language and purpose of reports. Apart from the availability and appeal of video reports, this activity helps students explore the language of oral reports and to think critically about the content included in the commentary.

---

**Input**

Teachers need to find a five-minute videotaped report documentary about a topic being studied by the class. Report documentaries are popular on television. They range from programs about wildlife species to those about ballet dancing. Television documentaries are also easy to come by and provide great models of reports.

---

**Procedure**

1. Show students a short video report on a topic they are studying, without the sound. It may be necessary to show the video more than once.

2. Lead students, either working in pairs or as a class to first compose orally, then in writing, a commentary to go with the video.

3. Allocate different lines of the commentary to individuals or pairs. Allow them to rehearse. Ask them to read the commentary as the videotape is played (sound off) a second time.

4. Encourage students to revise the commentary based on their experience with their first reading.

5. Play the video again with the sound on. Challenge pairs to compare the original commentary with the one they prepared, paying particular attention to language and content.

---

**Metacognitive Discussion**

1. What might be the differences between a written report and a report that accompanies a video?

2. What did you say in your report commentary that was not in the original?

3. Why did these differences occur?

---

**Closure**

Encourage students to share their commentary with the original producers of the video and with students in other classes.

# Written Language Activities

**Focus Activity**

# Report Reconstruction

**Report reconstruction** simply involves teachers selecting and photocopying a clear, topically organized report, cutting it up into its logical parts, such as Introduction, General Classification, the Body, and topical paragraph sections and having students reconstruct the text.

## Objective

This activity is designed to help students further develop their understanding of the structure and content of reports by physically manipulating chunks of a report text.

## Input

The teacher must select a report that uses compare-and-contrast and other top-level structures that can be physically separated for later reconstruction. Students enjoy this cooperative activity in which differences of opinion tend to emerge in regard to the sequence of topics and the quality of subheadings. The teacher must not be hasty about revealing the original text and should treat the differences of opinion as opportunities for learning. Each pair or group of students will need a copy of the cut-up text and basic knowledge of the subject being treated in the text.

## Procedures

1. Arrange students in groups of two to four.

2. Give a set of cut-up text pieces that comprise the whole original text to each group.

3. Tell students to reconstruct the text, devising subheadings as needed. (Note: If the text contains subheadings, you can either include or exclude them from the set students receive. If you exclude them, give students blank strips of paper on which they can write their proposed subheadings.)

4. Lead students to compare their topical reconstruction with the original and think critically about the whole text organization. Be sure to emphasize links between topics.

**Metacognitive Discussion**

1. If subheadings were available, how useful was it to have a foreshadowing of content?

2. If subheadings were not available, what difficulties arose through lack of a label for upcoming material?

3. What differences occurred between the original and the reconstructed text.

4. Might the new structure be superior?

**Closure**

Encourage students to exchange cut-up texts and see how the reconstructions compare. Prompt students to suggest topics that the author might have included in the original report and compare their subheadings with those of the author.

SkyLight Training and Publishing Inc.

**Focus Activity**  # Text Elaboration

**Text elaboration** is an activity that asks students to add information to an already written report.

## Objective

This activity provides students with an opportunity to think critically, expand on topic sentences, clarify paragraphs, and demonstrate their knowledge of a topic.

## Input

This activity requires that students have a good knowledge of a topic and so might best be used toward the end of a topic study. It also requires critical thinking to decide why particular information might have been left out. The teacher needs to obtain a report on a topic the class has studied and cut it into paragraphs. Each student group needs a set of the cut-up paragraphs.

## Procedure

1. Ask students to write an additional paragraph or two about the topic and to indicate the location of the new paragraph in the old text.
2. Direct groups to tape these paragraphs to the original and display them on a bulletin board.
3. Review the new text with the class and discuss whether it improved or deteriorated.

## Metacognitive Discussion

1. Why did you choose to place your paragraph in a particular position?
2. Why did you choose (among all possible topics) to include your topic?
3. How did you link your paragraph with the original paragraph? with the introduction to the report?

## Closure

Challenge students to share their new paragraphs with the class, and ask the class to note any new facts that emerged.

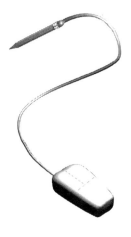

# WRITING Reports

CHAPTER 12

## Introduction to the Report Writing Model Program

The following thinking and writing report focus activities demonstrate how some of the focus activities in chapter 11 can be brought together in a program that might last several days.

A unit of study about conservation is the focus of the reports model program, tailored for the middle school or high school level. In particular, whales are the subject of study. The thinking frames that are introduced include brainstorm, meaning, and creative problem-solving frames; the writing frame is the problem-solving report writing frame. The types of thinking that are targeted are attributing and brainstorming, grouping, substantiating, justifying, classifying, observing, grouping, questioning, visualizing, personifying, clarifying, elaborating, comparing, sequencing, linking, and composing analogies.

The oral language objectives are to help students

1. solve problems;

2. present an oral report;

3. share information;

4. reach a consensus;

5. recall information;

6. develop social skills.

The exploring language objectives are to help students

1. explore the language choices made by the authors of reports;

2. identify the common conventions of reports;

3. use a report writing frame to jointly and independently construct a report.

The report thinking objectives are to help students

  1. construct brainstorm frames;

  2. construct meaning grids;

  3. construct creative problem-solving frames.

The science objectives for this unit are to help students

  1. identify the parts of a whale;

  2. understand the behavior of whales and their role in the ecosystem;

  3. understand the exploitation of the whale;

  4. understand cross-cultural perspectives about whales and the whaling industry

To prepare for this unit, teachers need to

  1. obtain books, videos, World Wide Web sites, Project Jonah resources, Greenpeace resources, and other documents about whales;

  2. organize teacher's aides and parents to assist during a trip to an aquarium, an oceanarium, or a museum that displays the skeleton or at least some bones from a whale. Prepare to have students view a presentation about whales;

  3. photocopy a single model report text about whales onto a transparency to display to the class;

  4. photocopy the problem-solution report writing frame (one per group and one on transparency for sharing with the class);

  5. photocopy brainstorm, creative problem-solving, and meaning frames (one per group and one on a transparency for sharing with the class).

As a reminder, the focus activities in this chapter are linked in a logical sequence for the program. Session numbers are used to show the sequence chosen, but some shifting may be appropriate for a particular class. Probably the activities in the working with writing frames and working with thinking frames sections are the most strongly linked.

# Building Knowledge of the Topic

**Focus Activity**   Visit

**Visit** a natural history museum. (Session 1)

---

**Objective**

Students build up their knowledge about whales before writing.

---

**Input**

The teacher has arranged a visit to a natural history museum with a display about whales. The activities associated with this visit may take more than one session either in the museum or back at class. The teacher needs to design a three-level guide (see fig. 12.1) following the visit.

---

**Procedure**

1. During the visit ask students to do the following things to build their knowledge of whales:

   a. View whale bones.

   b. View a movie and complete a three-level study guide (see fig. 12.1).

   c. Name parts of a whale.

   d. Talk about whales in the present tense.

   e. Summarize the history of whale exploitation.

   f. Name equipment associated with whale hunting through the ages.

2. Explain to students that they are to ask questions in class for which they have been unable to find answers.

3. Thank the curator, lecturer, or tour guide for the presentation.

4. During the visit, and later back at class, collect and combine students' initial responses so that the length and quality of what they say is extended.

# Model Three-Level Study Guide

### Three-Level Guide to Accompany the Movie or Trip

Circle your response.

**Level One: What was said and seen at the museum?**

Blue whales are more than 60 feet long.  Yes    No    Not Sure

**Level Two: What was meant by what was said and seen at the museum?**

By exhibiting a blue whale, people          Yes    No    Sometimes    Not Sure
will become more sympathetic to
their plight.

**Level Three: Would people at the museum agree that . . .**

Blue whales are the most valued          Yes    No    Sometimes    Not Sure
of the whale species.

*Figure 12.1*

## Metacognitive Discussion

What is the difference in the way you thought when answering Level One and Level Three questions on the Three-Level Study Guide?

## Closure

Pose this question to the class: How might we thank the museum staff for their help?

SkyLight Training and Publishing Inc.

**Focus Activity**    # Brainstorm

As a class, students complete a **brainstorm** thinking frame with the teacher, including asking about words, labels, and other questions. (Session 2)

---

**Objective**

This activity reminds students of what they know, helps them to share it with others, and gives the teacher some means to measure students' prior knowledge to illustrate their knowledge growth.

---

**Input**

The preferred option is for groups of four to six to have an enlarged brainstorm frame. Alternatively, the activity could be completed as a class with the teacher acting as scribe.

---

**Procedure**

1. First, lead students to complete the stages of the brainstorm frame.

   Stage 1. Collecting words

   Prompt students to list words related to the topic (in groups or as a class with you acting as scribe).

   Stage 2. Grouping words and labeling groups

   Ask or have the group leaders ask the following: Can we find two words in our collection that we think go together in some way?, Why do they go together?, and What are they both about? to finally provide the label.

   Stage 3. Enlarging groups

   Ask or have group leaders ask for other words that might be added under the label. Repeat stages 2 and 3.

   Stage 4. Questioning the unknown

   Lead students to make up questions based on the words and labels students don't know, and finally B.Y.O.Q. (bring your own questions).

   Stage 5. Researching questions

   Challenge students to suggest where they might find answers to their questions.

2. When the brainstorm frame is complete, explain how the brainstorm frame can be used to write a report. The labels can be used as subheadings for a report, although more

appealing subheadings would be welcome. The groups of words under the labels can provide key words (and correct spellings) for the topical paragraphs. Questions raise possibilities for further research and new sections for the report.

**Metacognitive Discussion**

What has this activity told us about our knowledge of the topic and about how to learn more?

**Closure**

Ask the class to suggest an appealing title for the brainstorm.

SkyLight Training and Publishing Inc.

**Focus Activity**  # Mailbox

The **mailbox** activity requires students to write questions about a topic, display them next to a mail box, try to answer each other's questions, and then post the answers for later collection and review. (Session 3)

### Objective

This activity engages students in designing questions that reflect what they do not know about a topic and in sharing information by answering other students' questions.

### Input

Students need some knowledge of the topic and need to be told that they should attempt to answer other students' questions. Teachers need to make mailboxes and provide paper on which students write their questions and answers.

### Procedure

1. Ask students to write questions about the topic (whales) and put their names on the papers.

2. Group similar questions and attach these and individual questions to mailboxes, one for each mailbox. Use silly putty or sticky glue to attach the questions.

3. Encourage students, individually or in pairs, to visit each mailbox, write answers to individual students, and post the answers in the mailbox.

4. Tell one group to empty each mailbox and distribute the answers. As an alternative, you may choose groups to compose summary answers for similar questions and then distribute the answers to all students.

### Metacognitive Discussion

1. How does designing questions about what you don't know help you learn?

2. Did you find the answers easy, hard, or incomplete?

### Closure

Remind students that this activity will be repeated during the course of the study. Tell students that they will select questions for inclusion in a final test.

**Focus Activity**

# Research

Students **research** using a variety of resources to investigate unanswered questions that arose as part of the brainstorm or mailbox activities. (Session 4)

### Objective

This reading to learn activity involves students using research questions to direct their reading.

### Input

The teacher needs to provide a range of print (books and internet) and visual resources (pictures, slides, videos) and know the resources well. Teachers will then be in a position to direct students to the resource(s) that will best answer their research questions.

### Procedure

1. Make sure students (working individually or in pairs) have a research question.
2. Review with the whole class how to check whether a resource might meet their needs (look at table of contents and index, scan chapters and subheadings).
3. Ask students to write their research questions at the top of a page and record notes under it.
4. After the note-collecting stage, ask students to write a short answer to their question.

### Metacognitive Discussion

1. What are the steps in answering a research question?
2. What step caused us most concern?
3. Collect some questions and decide if some might be more effective than others. Why are they more effective?

### Closure

Encourage students to share their questions and answers with the class.

**Focus Activity**

# Expressive Writing

**Expressive writing** uses a highlight of the museum visit as the basis for a brief expressive writing assignment. (Session 5)

## Objective

This activity involves students in identifying and focusing on one aspect of their visit, using draft writing skills, and deciding on the appropriate genre(s) to convey their meanings.

## Input

Remind students that any type of narrative, poetry, or factual text can be used. Review thinking strategies they might use prior to writing their text and draft writing skills such as writing on every second line and using invented spelling. Remind students that expressive writing is largely spontaneous and unrevised.

## Procedure

1. Tell students to identify one aspect of the trip to the natural history museum that they liked best.

2. Encourage students to select a thinking strategy to work on this experience before writing.

3. Instruct students to draft a written text. You must choose to have students to work in pairs and support each other in their writing. You may ask some to work with you and others to work independently.

## Metacognitive Discussion

This session allows students to apply their thinking and writing skills. They should be given plenty of opportunity to reflect on their success.

## Closure

Lead students to self-assess their thinking and writing and record this reflection in their writing folders, which become part of a portfolio assessment.

**Focus Activity** # Movement

In a **movement** activity, groups of students put together a short drama illustrating something they have learned about whales—often a mime plus commentary works best for these presentations. (Session 6)

## Objective

In this activity, students provide multiple representations of what they know and share these with the class. In the process, they should make new meanings (about whales).

## Input

In groups of six, students should select one aspect of the topic (for example, how humpback whales feed). The group might need a book that describes the selected aspect of the topic (feeding). The class should be introduced to the topic before the drama commences.

## Procedure

1. Direct students to select specific aspect of the topic and, using books supplied for the purpose, research, and write a text to accompany their performance. Ask them to plan a short (two-minute) presentation.

2. Encourage students to rehearse, then introduce, their topic to the class prior to the performance.

3. Tell students that during the performance, one student might read an extract from the book as the others mime the actions.

## Metacognitive Discussion

Ask each group what new understanding they gained through participating in the performance, and also, ask the same of the audience. Extend this to a discussion on how different ways of representing what we know result in new understandings.

## Closure

Lead the class to select one or two performances to share with another class.

SkyLight Training and Publishing Inc.

**Focus Activity**  Art

In an **art** activity, students contribute one thing that they know about whales to the production of a class mural. (Session 7)

### Objective

During this activity students are able to record their under-standing of a topic and teachers are able to assess students understanding.

### Input

A large sheet of paper and paints are required to complete a wall mural about whales. Students need to have progressed in their knowledge of whales to the point that they can contrib-ute a fact in the form of a drawing or label. Scissors and glue will be required to create the mural, together with marker pens for writing captions. It should be stressed to students that the illustration and written text should be accurate and detailed.

### Procedure

1. Arrange students in groups of two to four members.

2. Ask each group to select an object (such as whales), event (such as harpooning a whale), or idea (conservation of endangered species) to draw or cut out, glue on the mural, and eventually label.

3. Encourage students to add labels and giant whale bubbles where appropriate to help display the knowledge of whales that the class has gathered. (Note: Ask students to work individually so that you might have a means of assessing student achievement.)

### Metacognitive Discussion

Invite students to share how they researched before composing their illustration and text.

### Closure

Choose student volunteers to read their texts.

# Modeling Reports

**Focus Activity**

# Modeling Report Writing and Report Writing Frames

**Modeling report writing and report writing frames** gives teachers the opportunity to present well done reports to the students. Teachers model written reports, explaining their structure, tense, and literary devices, such as the use of analogy. (Session 8)

### Objective

By the completion of this session, students should know the conventions of a report text, and depending on their age, ways in which writers can be flexible within those conventions. They should also see how a report writing frame maps to the conventions of a report.

### Input

Teachers will need a transparency of one or more annotated (marking conventions) report texts, and students will need another report text to analyze in groups. They will also need a transparency of a report writing frame.

### Procedure

1. Read aloud several reports during the course of the unit.

2. Model the use of a report writing frame. Jointly construct part of the whale report with the class using a report writing frame appropriate to the experience and needs of the students. If this is the first time students have encountered reports, use the basic report writing frame.

3. Ask students, in groups, to analyze a new report and write labels indicating the conventions.

### Metacognitive Discussion

Ask students how knowing the conventions of a report might help them write one.

### Closure

Record while students list the conventions of a report, such as structure and literary devices.

# Working With Report Thinking Frames

 **Focus Activity**    # Introducing the Meaning Frame

**Introducing the meaning frame** is an activity that allows students to develop a frame that pulls together information before they begin writing. (Session 9)

## Objective

Students are helped to recognize an appropriate organization of meaning for a report.

## Input

The teacher needs an outline of a meaning frame and the labels developed in an earlier brainstorming activity (if available). Students working in groups need a meaning frame drawn up and ready to complete.

## Procedure

1. Arrange students in groups of four to six. Direct groups to begin a meaning frame by listing up to four types of whales across the top of the frame, then either:

   a. List labels from a brainstorm frame down the left side with plenty of spaces between for descriptors, then add descriptors; or

   b. list things known about each whale down the left side of the frame.

2. After students have completed the listing, ask them to share with the class. Then instruct them to complete the frame with either a check mark (yes, this whale has that characteristic); cross (no, this whale doesn't have that characteristic); period (sometimes yes, sometimes no); or question mark (we're not sure) in each square of the grid.

3. Tell students to analyze the rows and columns writing list and write comparative summary sentences.

## Metacognitive Discussion

Discuss with students how the meaning frame assisted them to learn.

## Closure

Encourage groups to review and share their best comparative summary sentence. Prompt students to reflect on how they will use the meaning frame in the future.

**Focus Activity** # Discussion and Research

Further **discussion and research** gives students the opportunity to discover and share information in the context of using a meaning frame. (Session 10)

## Objective

Inevitably, students will enter some question marks in the meaning frame (see session 9). The objective of this activity is to research answers to these questions.

## Input

Groups will need their meaning frames from session 9 and access to resources that might assist them to answer the questions.

## Procedure

1. Form groups to play jigsaw (see chapter 11), with the size of groups equal to the number of question marks on the meaning frames that remain unanswered.

2. Break students into expert jigsaw groups and ask each group to research one of these questions. For example, one group may research whether humpback whales migrate.

3. Tell students to report to their home groups what they have learned about their specialty question.

## Metacognitive Discussion

Discuss with students how the meaning frames helped them focus their research. Ask students to share the processes they used to research answers to their questions.

## Closure

Ask students to alter any question mark to a check mark or cross on their meaning frames, if the question has been answered by an expert jigsaw group.

# Working With Report Writing Frames

**Focus Activity**    # Expert Writing Exercise

**Expert writing exercise** builds on the specialist knowledge each student has developed during the jigsaw activity and other sessions. (Session 11)

---

**Objective**

This activity involves students in writing a report.

---

**Input**

Students will need an enlarged report writing frame and the research notes from sessions 9 and 10. Rather than writing an extensive report (about whales), students will focus on one aspect.

---

**Procedure**

1. Reconvene students in the expert jigsaw groups used in session 10.

2. Assign each expert group to use a report writing frame (according to students' ages and needs). Tell groups to jointly draft a section of a report based on their particular whale topic.

---

**Metacognitive Discussion**

Review the whole process of gathering and manipulating information that has occurred prior to this point and why this had to occur.

---

**Closure**

Challenge students to decide on the order reports should be given in class.

**Focus Activity** # Draft Writing Exercise

**Draft writing exercise** gives the class an opportunity to write together in small groups using the creative problem-solving frame. (Session 12)

## Objective

The objective of this activity is to use information generated from the use of a creative problem-solving frame to write a draft report.

## Input

A prerequisite for this activity is a topic-based problem. The teacher and students will need to identify and record as a question some problem involving whales. For example, How do we stop Japanese fishing crews from harpooning whales in the South Pacific? Students will need an enlarged creative problem-solving frame and an enlarged report writing frame appropriate to their ages and needs.

## Procedure

1. Lead the class, to begin to solve the problem using a creative problem-solving frame, limiting solution and evaluation to one only (fig. 16.18 and 16.19). A possible problem that might be used in the creative problem-solving frame is How do we stop countries from hunting whales?

2. Divide students into groups of three or four to complete their own creative problem-solving frame, using this or their own problem question.

3. Challenge each group member to draft a paragraph for a jointly constructed group report using a problem-solution paragraph structure. Tell them to base paragraphs on information generated within the creative problem-solving frame.

## Metacognitive Discussion

Discuss with students the advantages and disadvantages of the creative problem-solving, and gauge students' feelings on how they could use the creative problem-solving frame independently.

## Closure

Invite each group to report back to the class one way to stop countries from hunting whales.

**Focus Activity** # Writing a Report Independently

**Writing a report independently** asks students to prepare a report about whales based on their research. (Session 13)

## Objective

This activity provides teachers with an opportunity to measure students' abilities to write reports.

## Input

Students should have access to the report writing frame but need not use it. Students should see this activity as part of their and their teacher's language evaluation.

## Procedure

1. Before writing, work with the class to identify their purpose for writing and their audience(s). For example, students may decide that their purpose for writing is to communicate with Greenpeace, Project Jonah, politicians, parents, overseas government representatives, or the curator of the natural history museum.

2. Lead students to discuss how their selected audience might determine how and what they write.

3. Allow students to use one of the following options for writing (the last option is preferred):

   • Ask some students to draft on scraps of paper before conferring with you. Then ask them to transcribe their written text under a wall mural.

   • Ask some students to work in groups under your guidance to jointly construct a draft report, then complete a report independently.

   • Ask some students to complete whale fact sentences.

   • Ask some writers to compose reports independently.

4. Challenge students to revise and edit their writing.

5. Tell students to turn in their writing; then, if appropriate, have students send their reports to their chosen audience.

## Metacognitive Discussion

Review the thinking and writing processes introduced during this unit of work.

**Closure**

Encourage students to self-assess their report writing using the following criteria:

- Was the meaning clear?
- Was it well-structured?
- How well did I do with the spelling and punctuation?
- How confident am I about writing reports?

Tell students to also self-assess their use of report thinking frames and to analyze the effect that brainstorm, creative problem-solving, and meaning frames had on their writing.

SkyLight Training and Publishing Inc.

# Catch Them
# Thinking and Writing
# Explanations

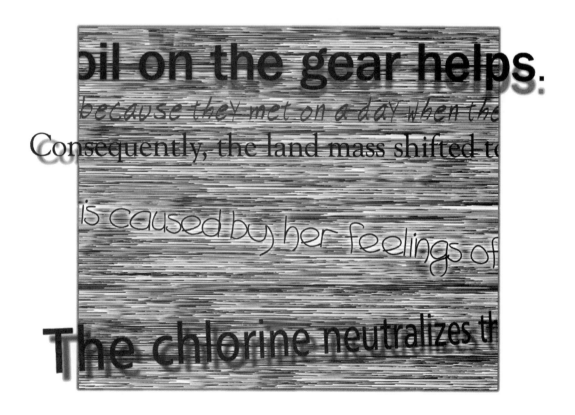

# Overview of Thinking and Writing Explanations

## Explanations are

Timeless

In the present tense

Event/process-ordered

## Writing explanations means using

Explanation Writing Frames

## Thinking explanations means using

Event Network Frames

Explanatory Sketch Board Frames

Analogy Frames

## Explanation thinking involves

| Sequencing | Inferencing |
|---|---|
| Generalizing | Composing cause and effect |
| Predicting | Drawing conclusions |
| Evaluating | |

## Types of explanations include

Mechanical

Technological

System

Natural

Narrative

SkyLight Training and Publishing Inc.

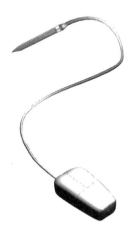

# WHAT IS an Explanation?

CHAPTER 13

The quick answer to the question of what is an explanation is that it is the kind of talking and writing that accounts for how something works or gives reasons for why something happens.

- When we explain how an automobile engine works, we give a *mechanical* explanation. When I explain how this computer I am using works, I give a *technological* explanation. Explaining to a friend how to order lunch is a *system* explanation and explaining how earthquakes happen is a *natural event* explanation.

- Other explanations give reasons for why things happen, like why people get depressed, why we have global warming, why the moon looks full, or why we need food.

Unlike a description or report that may be about static things, an explanation is always about a dynamic process—what is going on.

Explanations are common to science because part of scientific meaning is captured by explaining how things behave—as well as what they are made of, which is typical of a description or report. Other explanations are more personal, such as Explain why you haven't done your homework.

In contrast to reports that focus on defining and classifying things, explanations focus on processes. Often this means using a logical, step-by-step, cause-and-effect sequence to explain the process, an organization that says this happened because that happened. Diagrams are commonly used to make these processes clearer.

The events and processes described in an explanation are logically ordered in an implication sequence. This simply means that one event, such as holding a flame under ice, has implications for the next thing that happens, that is, the ice melting. Without the first event in the sequence, the second event would not happen. Writers signal these implication sequences using such words as *because, as a result, consequently, so, and then,* and *this causes.*

Because explanations are about how and why things happen, they contain many action verbs, and like reports, explanations talk about generic things (e.g., atoms, not a particular atom).

The way scientists write explanations is changing. In the past, scientists would typically use passive sentences. For example, they would write: The crystals were dissolved by the hot water instead of placing the action up front as in the sentence The hot water dissolved the crystals. Today, scientists use a more active style, write in the first person, and hedge rather than sounding totally convinced. For example, they might say "I think this was caused by . . . ." The conventions of factual texts are always in a state of change. In summary, explanations most often

- say how something works or why something happens

- use the present tense

- begin by stating something general about the thing (phenomenon) to be explained, followed by a logical sequence of events that form the explanation

- include words that signal time relationships, such as *first, next* (like a narrative)

- use a lot of action verbs

- use generalized subjects (like a report)

There is no pure explanation. In science, explanations are often embedded in longer mixed texts describing experiments. Explanations are also embedded in descriptions and reports—after all, if you want to describe the eye, at some stage you need to explain how it works.

Explanations also come in narrative form as myths. This type of explanation may explain why the stars twinkle and how mountains came to be where they are.

Explanations and narratives intersect in the form of reflective writing. This type of writing, sometimes seen in diaries, allows students to step back and analyze experiences and so more clearly explain to themselves why or how something happened. (For example, a writer may ask himself, "Why did she walk away from me?")

# Why Think and Write Explanations?

When students explain, they are accounting for how something works and are setting out the causal links between one event and another. This might be done in a single sentence (e.g., I'm happy because I've just won a million dollars)—or in a series of sentences.

Explanations in the form of reflections help students explain to themselves, and sometimes to others, a new understanding that has been reached through connecting something recently observed with old knowledge. Sometimes, these reflections express a personal point of view, as in learning logs. Explanations are often the kind of text we compose after using other types of texts, such as narratives, procedures, and reports. Clearly, observation (a component of narratives) tends to precede the writing of explanations.

Explanations are tricky to compose because they demand that students infer and that they see not always obvious connections between events. Often, this kind of thinking requires students to image because the connections are, literally, not clear. For example, an explanation of why ice melts may require an image of things that are hidden from direct observation. This is not to say that Grade 1 students should avoid talking and writing explanations. Helping students get in touch with the scientific theories inside their heads and expressing these to the teacher is a crucial first step in the learning-teaching process.

# What Does an Explanation Look and Sound Like?

Explanations come in a variety of types. Here are some types of explanation and examples of those types.

Mechanical Explanations

- How an automobile engine works
- How airplanes fly

Technological Explanations

- How a telephone works
- Why and how a lightning rod works

System Explanation

- Explain the water cycle
- How airports control air traffic

Natural Explanation

- How snakes kill their prey
- Why you see the lightning before hearing the thunder

Narrative Explanation

- Explain natural occurrences in narrative form, often giving life or spirit to objects and events

Figures 13.1 to 13.6, which are models of explanations, share similar conventions. Teachers may want to discuss these models and a range of other explanations including myths, to encourage students to identify conventions of explanations.

The conventions of these models may not be obvious to students. Although it is important that they have some idea of what explanations look and sound like, the conventions should never be used prescriptively. The phenomenon, general explanation, elaboration, and restatement labels found in the model explanations serve to guide, not prescribe.

When students write myths or explanations, encourage them to use words that signal the sequence of events and the relationships between events. The words *and, and then, because, so, and so, as a result, as a consequence, since,* and *if* are useful in this respect.

Indigenous explanations were often in the form of myths (see fig. 13.7). There are a number of differences between a natural explanation and a myth. For example, if the myth in figure 13.7 had been written as a natural explanation,

- the summary or conclusion would be at the beginning and serve to state what was to be explained;
- the setting and the initiating event would be replaced with the general explanation;
- the action-outcome episodes would be represented by event sequences;
- the talking animals would be replaced with nonhuman things like air, stars, and rocks;
- the tense would be changed from the past to the present.

# How Do We Start Thinking and Writing Explanations?

## What Are Explanation Writing Frames?

Explanation writing frames (see fig. 13.8) provide students with a shape for draft writing. The main features of explanations are signaled by subheadings that remind students of the kind of meanings that might be made at that point in the text. This frame is not designed to usurp the writing process but rather to support it.

### How to Introduce the Explanation Writing Frame

Typically, during a science lesson or any lesson that involves explanation thinking, teachers encourage students to write expressively before using an explanation writing frame. Expressive writing is a spontaneous means of writing to learn. It involves working through a possible explanation for what happened, and it is the writing that occurs at key points

# Model Natural Explanation: Basic

**How Flies Walk Upside Down**

**Phenomenon** (This is the thing you are going to explain.)

Flies can walk on ceilings.

**General Explanation** (This is where you provide some background information to the reader.)

This is because they have special pads on the soles of their feet.

**Explanation**

These pads are covered with tiny hairs. At the tip of each hair is a drop of "glue." The glue helps the fly walk on the ceiling.

**Restatement**

This is partly why flies can walk on ceilings. Can you think of other reasons?

*Figure 13.1*

# Model Natural Explanation: Expanded

**How a Star Dies**

**Phenomenon** (This is the thing you are going to explain.)

Stars die when they explode, and this is how scientists think it happens.

**Explanation**

*(Event 1)*

Stars are like slowly exploding hydrogen bombs. When a star uses up all its hydrogen, gravity pulls all its atoms together.

*(Event 2)*

**When this happens**, huge amounts of energy are released.

*(Event 3)*

**As a result**, stars blow themselves apart in one final bright explosion.

*(Event 4)*

**Finally**, the glowing gas from the outer part of an exploded star speeds off into space and, **consequently**, the brightness fades into the darkness of space.

**Restatement**

That is how scientists think stars die.

*Figure 13.2*

# Model Natural Explanation: Why?

**Shaking the Plates: What Causes Earthquakes?**

**Phenomenon** (This is the thing you are going to explain.)

When the earth moves suddenly, you may feel an earthquake. But how does this happen?

**General Explanation** (This is where you provide some background information to the reader.)

The earth's crust is made up of huge, slowly moving tectonic plates. Some are pulling apart, others are sliding past each other, and some are colliding and pushing up mountains. Most earthquakes occur along the boundaries of these plates.

## Explanation

*(Event 1)*

In fact, earthquakes are caused by the movement of these plates. As tectonic plates move and collide with each other, they put great strain on rocks in the earth's crust. Sometimes, the strain between the plates becomes so great that these rocks suddenly snap apart and move into new positions. When that happens, the energy released sends shock waves for long distances through the rocks, causing the ground to shudder, shake, and even tear apart.

*(Event 2)*

When the ground tears apart, a fault is formed, and, once there is a fault in the earth's crust, movement, which we feel as earthquakes, happens along the fault line. The rocks on either side of the fault are rough, so they do not slip pass each other smoothly. There is a lot of friction between these rocks and, for movement to take place, the strain must build up until it is released in the form of an earthquake.

## Restatement

This is how we think earthquakes occur, but we have more to find out.

*Figure 13.3*

# Model Mechanical Explanation

## High and Dry: How A Floating Dock Works

**Phenomenon** (This is the thing you are going to explain.)

Ever thought about how big ships are taken out of the water for painting and repair? Well, some are raised high and dry on a floating dock.

**General Explanation** (This is where you provide some background information to the reader.)

A floating dock is a floating platform for holding ships. The sides and floor are hollow and divided into several separate tanks. The dock can be sunk into the water until it is low enough for a ship to float in, and then the dock is raised until the ship is high and dry. This is how a floating dock works.

## Explanation

*(Event 1)*

When water is let into the bottom of the tanks, air is allowed to escape out valves in the top. As a result, the dock becomes less buoyant and sinks. When the valves are shut, the remaining air is trapped in the tanks. This stops any more water from entering the tanks, therefore, the dock stops sinking.

*(Event 2)*

To raise a floating dock, air is pumped into the tanks. This forces water out the bottom. As a consequence, the dock becomes more buoyant and rises out of the water.

(Event 3)

By carefully opening and closing the valves and working the pumps, the dock can be kept level as it goes up and down.

## Restatement

It's amazing how air in a floating dock can be used to raise and lower a huge ship.

*Figure 13.4*

SkyLight Training and Publishing Inc.

# Model Technology Explanation

### Strike One: How a Lightning Rod Works

**Phenomenon** (This is the thing you are going to explain.)

A thunderstorm can be dangerous but lightning rods protect us and our property.

**General Explanation** (This is where you provide some background information to the reader.)

Lightning can be seen as a brilliant flash of light that results from an electrical discharge between clouds, or between a cloud and the earth. If a lightning discharge hits a building, it may cause damage. If it strikes people, they may be killed.

A lightning rod helps to prevent lightning and protects buildings and people if lightning should strike. This is how a lightning rod works.

## Explanation

*(Event 1)*

Thunderstorms create strong negative charges at the base of thunderclouds. As a result, these cause strong positive charges on the ground below. (Positives and negatives attract each other like opposite ends of a magnet.)

*(Event 2)*

Lightning rods can help prevent lightning strikes. One end of the rod is placed in the ground, the other is placed above the tallest point on a building. During a thunderstorm, positive charges from the earth travel up the rod to the top and flow upward off the rod, thus reducing the negative charge in the thundercloud.

*(Event 3)*

A lightning rod also helps protect buildings and people. If lightning strikes, it tends to hit the rod, flows down the cable, and passes into the ground without causing damage.

## Restatement

The noise of a thunderstorm might scare you, but a lightning rod can protect you and buildings from harm.

*Figure 13.5*

SkyLight Training and Publishing Inc.

# Model Systems Explanation
## The Water Cycle

**Phenomenon** (This is the thing you are going to explain.)

Did you know that the earth has always had about the same amount of water? That is because water is part of a never-ending cycle. Three things are caught up in this cycle: air, heat from the sun, and, of course, water.

## Explanation

Although there is no beginning and no end to the water cycle, this explanation begins with water evaporating from rivers, lakes, oceans, soil, and animals.

*(Event 1)*

The heat of the sun changes water into water vapor, a sort of wet gas that makes the air humid.

*(Event 2)*

Because water vapor is warmer than the surrounding air, it rises into the sky, cools, and condenses into clouds.

*(Event 3)*

Clouds then carry the water vapor around until it is cool enough for the water vapor to condense as drizzle (small water droplets), rain, or, if the vapor gets very cold, snow.

Now the cycle is ready to continue as water is evaporated again.

## Restatement

Just think, because of the water cycle, the water you swim in today may be the water that falls from the sky as rain tomorrow.

*Figure 13.6*

SkyLight Training and Publishing Inc.

# Model Explanation: Myth

**Why There Are Shooting Stars (Native American Myth)**

**Setting [Time, Characters]** (In an explanation, this is where you state the thing you are going to explain.)

A long time ago, Coyote was a great dancer. More than anything, he liked to dance.

**Initiating Event** (In an explanation, this is Event 1.)

At nighttime, Coyote looked up at the dancing stars and said to himself, "I should like to dance with the stars."

**Action and Outcome Event** (In an explanation, this is Event 2.)

Coyote waited at the top of a high hill until the stars started to dance. "Let me dance with you," Coyote called out. But the stars only laughed.

**Action and Outcome Event** (In an explanation, this is Event 3.)

"I am a great dancer . . . Let me dance with you," Coyote called out again.
The stars asked one another, "What do you say?"

**Complication and Solution Event** (In an explanation, this is Event 4.)

The red star asked, "How can he dance with us when he is on earth and we are in the sky?"
The south star suggested that one of them reach down and hold onto Coyote's paw. So the south star reached down and Coyote stretched his paws toward the star.

**Action and Outcome Event** (In an explanation, this is Event 5.)

The south star caught one paw and swung Coyote through the sky, dancing faster and faster until Coyote was tired. Coyote wanted to stop dancing but the star danced even faster, until Coyote could not see or catch his breath.
"I am ready to stop dancing," Coyote said, but the star laughed and danced faster. Coyote's paw slipped, and he fell through the air. When he hit the ground, he made a great hole in the earth and was never seen again.

**Summary** (This is replaced by a Restatement in an explanation.)

To this day, Coyote's brothers still try to dance with the stars. Whenever we see a shooting star, legend has it that it is Coyote falling through the sky.

*Figure 13.7*    Adapted from "Why There Are Shooting Stars" as retold by Natalia Belting, from *The Earth Is on a Fish's Back: Tales of Beginnings* by Natalia Belting; Henry Holt and Company, 1965.

# Explanation Writing Frame

An explanation tells us how something works or gives reasons why something happens.

The title of my explanation is _____

## Say what you are going to explain.

_____

_____

_____

_____

## Write a brief general explanation.

Write how or why some object or system works or write why something occurs.

_____

_____

_____

_____

## Give more detail about the thing you are explaining.

Put events in the right order. Make clear links between each event.

_____

_____

_____

_____

## Restatement

Say again what it is you have explained. You might begin with This is why . . . , or This is how . . . .

_____

_____

_____

_____

*Figure 13.8*

during a lesson. Expressive explanations may be recorded by pairs of students on clipboards or in an explanation thinking log. The explanations recorded are likely to be tentative and approximate.

The use of expressive writing is consistent with a generative approach to learning that respects students' emerging theories as the basis for new learning and sees danger in imposing expert views on students who have not yet generated the links between what they know and the new explanation. The generative approach is illustrated in the burning focus activities in the model explanation writing program discussed in chapter 15. These activities encourage frequent writing-to-learn experiences, together with the opportunity for students to record their understanding of a concept (such as floating and sinking) as a written explanation toward the end of the investigation.

Explanation writing frames also offer students opportunities to further develop their theories as to how or why something happens, but in a more formal frame than that used during expressive writing.

Further, between expressive writing and the use of an explanation writing frame, teachers are encouraged to use event network frames, sketch board frames, and analogy frames to help writers to further think through their experiences. These ways of thinking are important for students who are required by the writing frame to "Give more detail about the thing you are explaining" (see fig. 13.8).

## Assessing and Reflecting on Explanation Writing Frames

The writing component of the program needs to be assessed by both teachers and students. To assist teachers to monitor and record students' progress, an explanation writing assessment rubric is provided (see fig. 13.9).

Summative assessments (the "where is each child at right now" type of assessment) will be required from time to time. However, the focus in the rubric in figure 13.9 is on formative assessment, using a continuum to record development. Any assessment placed at the left end of the arrow indicates the child is still dependent on the teacher to achieve this behavior. An assessment placed to the right indicates the learner is consistently independent in achieving this behavior. Teachers may choose to date the arrow when they see examples of specific behaviors. Students are encouraged to use the rubric for self-assessment.

## What Are Explanation Thinking Frames?

The purpose of an explanation thinking frame is to help students prepare to talk or write explanations. These frames engage students in explanation thinking, which contrasts with the kind of thinking required to compose, for example, a persuasive argument.

# Assessing Explanation Writing

|  | Dependent | Independent |
|---|---|---|

## Meaning

Enough information ⟷

Clearly expressed ⟷

Keeps to topic ⟷

Has voice ⟷

Achieves purpose ⟷

Shows logical approach ⟷

## Structure

Phenomenon ⟷

General explanation ⟷

Explanation (Events) ⟷

Elaboration ⟷

Links signaled ⟷

Present tense ⟷

Paragraphed ⟷

Restatement ⟷

## Explanation Forms

Mechanical ⟷

Technological ⟷

System ⟷

Natural ⟷

Narrative (myths) ⟷

## Uses Explanation Draft Writing Frame

Uses all parts ⟷

Includes other forms of writing in explanation    Yes    No

No longer needs to use explanation writing frames    Yes    No

*Figure 13.9*

SkyLight Training and Publishing Inc.

The following frames are designed to help students think in clever, and to some extent, unnatural ways prior to crafting an explanation. Initially, these frames are used as teaching frames, that is, the teacher uses them with students to help them think explanations. Later, these frames become student or learner frames as students learn to use them independently.

The following explanation thinking frames are described:

- Event network frames
- Sketch board frames
- Analogy frames

## What Is the Event Network Frame?

Event networks are frames within which students can diagrammatically record explanations of how or why something happens by identifying interacting states and events. This frame includes a key question at the top of the frame, a diagram illustrating a process, and a summary statement at the bottom of the frame.

For example, in figure 13.10, the diagram includes circles that represent natural states, that is, the state of water warmer than the air, and the state of water vapor in the air. The arrows represent events that move the states from one to another and indicate the direction of change. Above the arrow is a label that indicates the thing that happened or events (in this case evaporation) that occurred between states. Note that, in the summary statements, the text is written in the present tense, not *will evaporate* but *evaporates*.

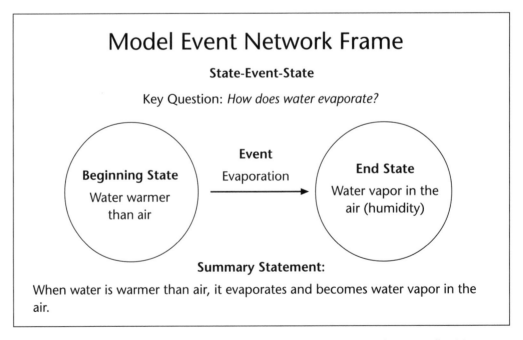

*Figure 13.10*    Adapted from "The Discourse of Geography," S. Eggins, J. R. Martin, and P. Wignell, 1987.

After the event network frame has been drawn, students write a summary statement describing the process. Note in figure 13.10 how other key explanation signal words might be used: When water is warmer than air, it evaporates and *changes into/turns into/transforms into* water vapor in the air. These signal words convey the process nature of any explanation.

In figure 13.11, the beginning state takes up where the previous network finished. This event network includes multiple events and states, shown as a midpoint. The key question is How do clouds form? and, as illustrated, three events are central to this explanation.

In figure 13.12, one of these events, adiabatic cooling, is further explained. This figure shows the process of adiabatic cooling, so the event network needs to put a thing, in this case air, on each arrow. Note also that an outcome of the middle process is energy, which is also recorded as a thing. This event network presents a picture of a process with things as the mediating steps. Figures 13.10 and 13.11 show states changed by events.

It is worth saying that the event network presents events in two roles: one as a mediator between two states and one as the object affected by a state or thing. Choosing which event network to use depends to some extent on where the emphasis of the explanation lies. If the purpose is to show that something becomes something else, the state-event-state model seems most appropriate e.g., ice-heat-water); if the purpose is to show how a process works, the event-state-event seems a good choice (e.g., adiabatic cooling-air-clouds).

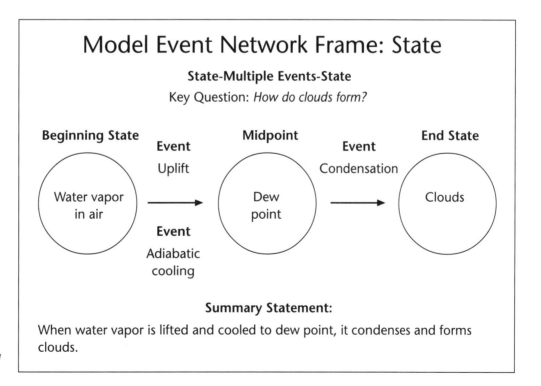

*Figure 13.11*

### Model Event Network Frame: State

**State-Multiple Events-State**
Key Question: *How do clouds form?*

**Beginning State** — **Event** Uplift / **Event** Adiabatic cooling — **Midpoint** — **Event** Condensation — **End State**

Water vapor in air → Dew point → Clouds

**Summary Statement:**
When water vapor is lifted and cooled to dew point, it condenses and forms clouds.

SkyLight Training and Publishing Inc.

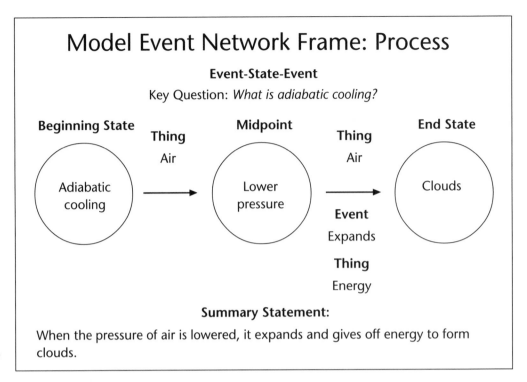

*Figure 13.12*

*Using the Event Network Frame*

Begin by modeling and discussing simple changes of a natural state. For example, how ice as a solid can change into a liquid and then into a gas. Then ask students to think about what the flame and heat might be doing to the ice—to form a visual image of this process and to sketch what they see. Encourage students to share and talk about their sketches.

Then ask students in groups to design an event network based on one change of state. This sequence—mental images, sketched image, talk, and finally, writing—within an event network frame is crucial to learning. The multiple representations and successive levels of abstraction help students come to terms with complex and abstract processes typical of those presented in explanations.

Now, use an envoy strategy in which individuals move to other groups and share their home group's completed event network frame. Finally, have the students use the completed event network frames to jointly compose written explanations.

## What Is the Explanatory Sketch Board Frame?

The explanatory sketch board frame (see fig. 13.13) is designed to help students sort out cause-and-effect meanings that are central to any explanation of how or why something occurs. The frame helps in two ways: first, by requiring students to represent and expand on what they know verbally and visually; and second, by making clear, graphically, the links between the events that make up an explanation as the links are drawn in the sketch board storyboard.

The sketch board frame is used to sequence and elaborate events prior to writing an explanation. Teachers might begin by listing process events in order. If there are six such events, the teacher might form six groups of students, who draw an explanation of one event each. A modified form of the envoy procedure can be used at this point, with half the group moving to another group to explain their sketches. When students return to their home groups, they jointly compose a caption that explains the process they have drawn. The sketches and captions are then displayed and the teacher works with the whole class to jointly construct links between the sketches.

### *Using the Explanatory Sketch Board Frame*
The procedure for using an explanatory sketch board frame (see fig. 13.13) is described within the context of a scientific study of floating and sinking. (See fig. 13.14 for creating another example showing why a balloon rises.) Students go through the following process as they put the explanatory sketch board frame to use:

1. Students share "before" views in respect to the investigation. For example, I think that things made from metal will not float on water because . . . .

2. The teacher and students outline an investigation. For example, Try to float this needle on the water.

3. Students share and record predictions (expressive explanation writing).

4. The teacher models how to use an explanatory sketch board frame, then proceeds with the investigation.

5. Students share "after" investigation views. For example, I now think that things made from metal will or might float on water if . . . because . . . when . . . .

6. Students, working with partners, complete the explanation sketch board frame to explain what happened in the investigation, that is, why the needle was able to float or why it sank.

8. Students share and discuss these explanations as a class.

9. If necessary, based on the class discussion, students modify their sketches and add a written explanation below each sketch.

For a complex investigation, students might produce a series of sketches explaining what happened at each stage of the investigation. The teacher should encourage students to successively modify their sketches.

# Model Explanatory Sketch Board Frame

**Why a Hot-Air Balloon Rises**

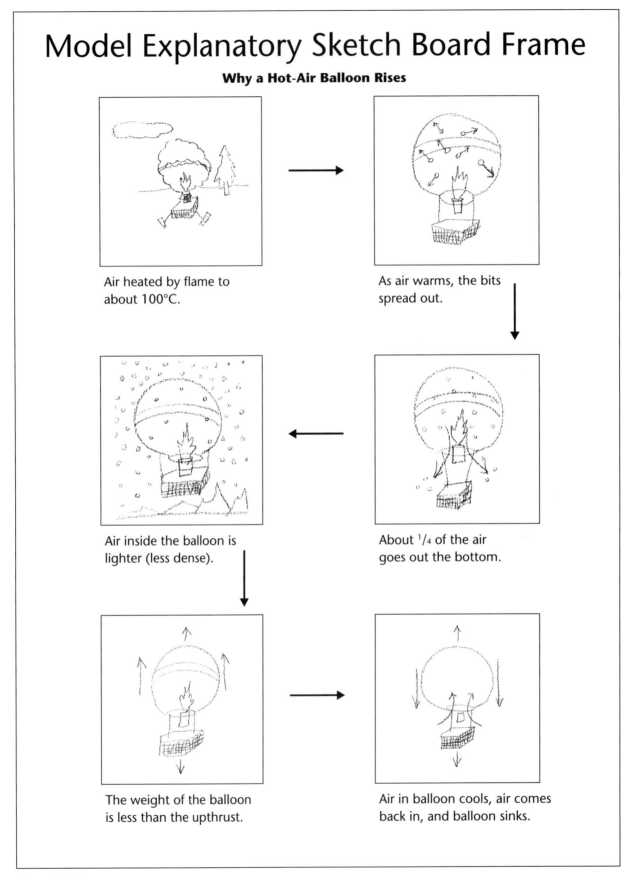

Air heated by flame to about 100°C.

As air warms, the bits spread out.

Air inside the balloon is lighter (less dense).

About ¼ of the air goes out the bottom.

The weight of the balloon is less than the upthrust.

Air in balloon cools, air comes back in, and balloon sinks.

*Figure 13.13*

SkyLight Training and Publishing Inc.

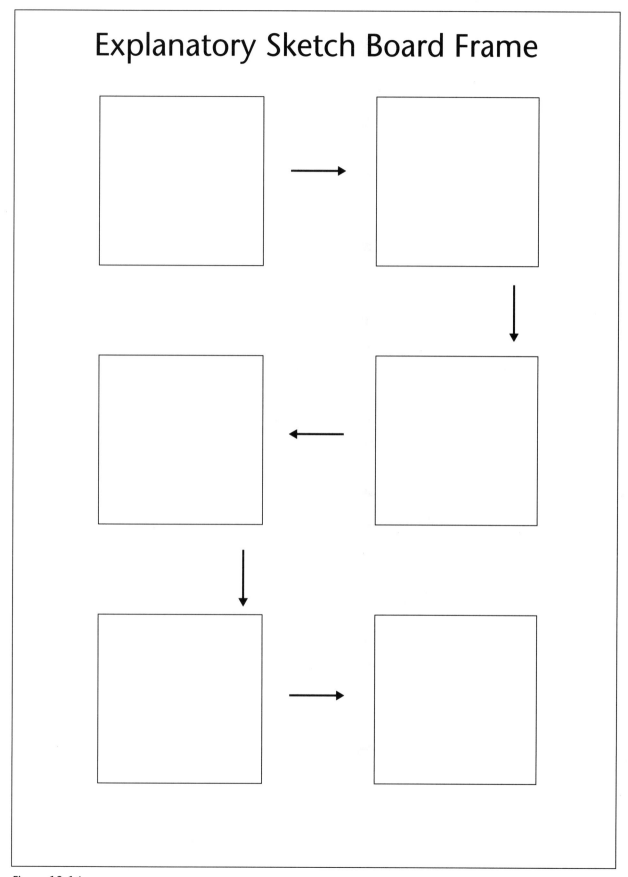

# Explanatory Sketch Board Frame

*Figure 13.14*

## What Is the Analogy Frame?

An analogy frame (see fig. 13.15) provides students with a means of linking new concepts to existing knowledge through the construction of analogies. It further allows students to examine the adequacy of their analogies, thus further defining the new concept or process.

Analogies tend to evoke visual images that are crucial to students because they peg the new concept in memory and are often the only way to see something that is not available to direct inspection (such as the motion of water molecules as they are heated).

### Using the Analogy Frame

As an introduction, prior to using the procedure listed below, students might first write one-liners to identify the two parts of the analogy. For example,

- The heart is like a force pump.

- The eye is like a camera.

- Photosynthesis is like baking bread. (Both are food-making processes in which the ingredients are combined and converted by energy.)

- An electric circuit works like a water circuit.

Later any one of these can be expanded using a modified matched concept list (refer back to chapter 10, see fig. 10.16). For example, the eye is like a camera . . .

| *Camera* | *Eye* |
|----------|-------|
| lens | lens |
| aperture | pupil |
| diaphragm | iris |
| film | retina |

This introduction prepares students for the full analogical frame, which is introduced over several lessons.

To complete an analogy frame (see fig. 13.16), teachers

- introduce the key concept and give a brief description or explanation;

- introduce the analogy, discuss it to insure all students understand the analogy concept, then complete the description;

- identify and record the relevant features of the analogy;

- identify and record the similarities between the analogy and the key concept;

- identify and record where the analogy breaks down;

- orally, then in writing, jointly with students summarize important aspects of the key concept.

# Model Analogy Frame

The event to be explained is an earthquake.

**1.** **Associated Events**

Seismic waves

**Description**

Shock waves through the earth

**2.** **Analogy**

Wobbly Jell-O

**Description**

When you shake Jell-O it ripples on top.

**3.** **Relevant Features of Analogy**

The earth moves like the surface of Jell-O during an earthquake.

**4.** **Similarities**

Both can be distorted.

Both crack when shaken.

Both move up and down in a wave-like motion.

**5.** **Differences**

The earth is made up of rock, sand, and clay, but Jell-O is the same consistency throughout.

**6.** **Summary**

A seismic wave occurs when the earth shakes causing the ground to move up and down and to crack.

*Figure 13.15*

# Analogy Frame

The event to be explained is_____

1.  **Associated Events**              **Description**

    _____            _____
    _____            _____
    _____            _____

2.  **Analogy**                        **Description**

    _____            _____
    _____            _____
    _____            _____

3.  **Relevant Features of Analogy**

    _____
    _____
    _____

4.  **Similarities**

    _____
    _____
    _____

5.  **Differences**

    _____
    _____
    _____

6.  **Summary**

    _____
    _____
    _____

*Figure 13.16*

SkyLight Training and Publishing Inc.

## Assessing and Reflecting on Explanation Thinking Frames

The assessment rubric for explanation thinking frames is shown in figure 13.17. It may be presented after each frame has been introduced or after all the frames have been introduced. As with the other rubrics for assessment, it is intended for formative assessment, using a continuum from dependent on the thinking frame to independent of the thinking frame.

# Assessing Explanation Thinking

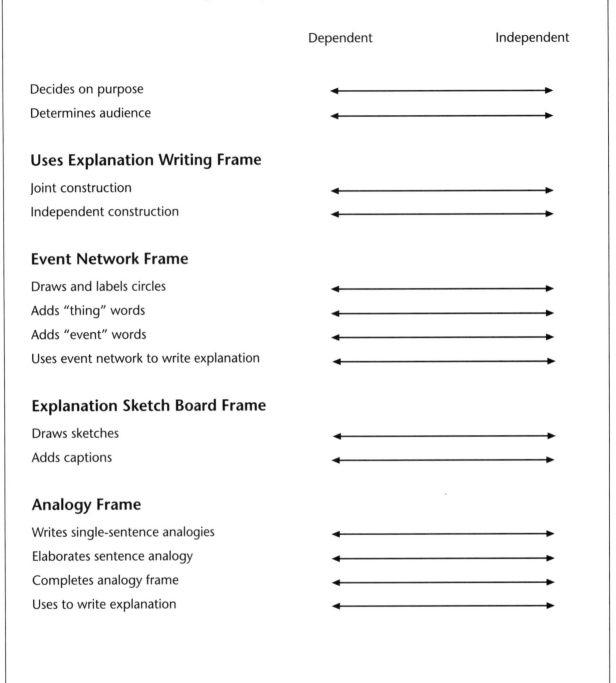

Dependent                              Independent

Decides on purpose

Determines audience

**Uses Explanation Writing Frame**

Joint construction

Independent construction

**Event Network Frame**

Draws and labels circles

Adds "thing" words

Adds "event" words

Uses event network to write explanation

**Explanation Sketch Board Frame**

Draws sketches

Adds captions

**Analogy Frame**

Writes single-sentence analogies

Elaborates sentence analogy

Completes analogy frame

Uses to write explanation

*Figure 13.17*

SkyLight Training and Publishing Inc.

# PRACTICE ACTIVITIES
## to Support Thinking and Writing Explanations

CHAPTER 14

## Oral Language Activities

**Focus Activity** # Buzz Groups

In **buzz groups**, student complete sentences by adding either the cause or the effect to the topic of the sentence.

### Objective

This activity helps students construct sentences that contain causal statements and causal inferences.

### Input

Students are seated in groups of four to six and elect a leader and reporter. Students are reminded that explanations often tell why or how something happens and that they are to think of creative explanations to complete the sentences. Students will be asked to share their "best" sentences.

### Procedure

Use the following activity to add the *cause*:

1. Seat students in a circle, in groups of 4 to 6 members.

2. Ask each student in each group to complete the following sentences (as imaginatively or factually as possible):

   a. The girl was late for school because . . . .

   b. The Mars Pathfinder was able to land on Mars because . . . .

3. Explain that after each sentence the group should select the best explanation and the reporter will share it with the class.

Use the following activity to construct *effect* explanations:

1. Seat students in their groups.

2. Each student completes the following sentences (as imaginatively or factually as possible):

   a. She didn't eat all day so . . . .

   b. The girl went out in the rain without her coat and . . . .

3. Explain that after each sentence, the group should select the best explanation and the reporter will share it with the class.

## Metacognitive Discussion

Apart from voting on the best explanations, guide students to identify the word or words that began their explanations. Recall any explanation that required more than one event.

## Closure

Lead groups to record their best explanations and underline the word or words that signaled the beginning of the explanations (e.g., because, etc.).

**Focus Activity** # Explanation Show-and-Tell

In **explanation show-and-tell**, students bring an object to class and explain how it works.

## Objective

This activity helps students produce oral explanations.

## Input

Rather than students talking about an object, the teacher challenges them in advance (perhaps for a week's worth of show-and-tells) to bring an object to class and explain how it works. It could be anything from a clock to the motor of a lawn mower. This activity must be accompanied by input from the teacher who models oral explanations by presenting several show-and-tells. Students will improve these explanations if they are reminded to ask questions about anything that was not explained in sufficient detail and if the groups are supportive at the rehearsal stage.

## Procedure

1. In advance, ask students to bring an object for their show-and-tell.

2. Divide students into groups with (at least) one object for show-and-tell per group. Encourage students to rehearse an explanation show-and-tell with their group. (Note: Groups must be supportive and help speakers with their explanations.)

3. Prompt students to present their explanations to the whole class.

## Metacognitive Discussion

What suggestions were you able to give the speaker which further improved his or her explanation show-and-tell?

## Closure

Choose students to present an explanation for the next class. Depending on the age of the students, lead the class to identify what kinds of explanation (natural, system, technological, mechanical, or narrative) were presented.

# Visual Language Activities

**Focus Activity** # Explanatory Sketch Board

This activity uses an **explanatory sketch board** to help students generate images depicting their explanations.

## Objective

This activity involves students visualizing a process, then presenting an oral explanation based on their sketches and images.

## Input

Teachers need to find a simple, short explanation. Students need an explanatory sketch board frame that has one event or reason box per event, which provides reasons for what happens in the explanation. (Note: As students gain proficiency with this activity, they can decide on how many boxes are required after a first reading of the explanation.)

## Procedure

1. Read aloud a short, simple explanation. (Note: You can provide students with explanatory sketch board frames with the required number of event or reason boxes, or you can ask students to draw the right number of boxes after the first reading.)

2. Read the explanation a second time, event by event. Between each event pause long enough for students to draw a sketch of what happened in the explanation. Continue until you have read the complete explanation.

3. Prompt students to describe each sketch (and provide the associated explanation) to a partner.

4. Name each event for the class and ask the students to picture in their heads what happened. (Note: Make sure students' sketches are concealed at this stage.)

## Metacognitive Discussion

1. Why is it necessary to sketch and image an explanation? (Answer: Because often the "things" in an explanation are abstract or unavailable for direct inspection.)

2. What new understanding did you gain from sketching and imaging?

**Closure**

Challenge student volunteers to share their explanations, orally, with the class. Have them display their explanatory sketch boards in a learning center in the classroom.

# Written Language Activities

**Focus Activity** ## Passive and Active Voice

In **passive and active voice**, students practice changing sentences from the active to passive voice and identifying the use of the passive voice in authentic explanations.

### Objective

This activity requires students to describe and become proficient with the active and passive voice.

### Input

A convention of most written explanations, especially in the past and in more scholarly publications, was to use the passive voice. Following are examples of active and passive voice:

*Active Voice:* The pressure fractured the earth.

*Passive Voice:* The earth was fractured by the pressure.

*Active Voice:* The earthquake killed 300 people.

*Passive Voice:* Three hundred people were killed by the earthquake.

Teachers need a number of sentences in the passive voice for display on an overhead projector or on a chalkboard. Students need to understand the difference between passive and active voice.

### Procedure

1. Ask students to work in pairs or independently.

2. Display sentences in the passive voice on the overhead or the chalkboard.

3. Prompt students to rewrite the sentences in the active voice, taking care to identify the subject, verb, and object for each sentence.

4. Direct students to share their rewritten sentences with another pair or another student.

### Metacognitive Discussion

1. How do you speak on the playground? Do you use active or passive sentences?

2. Why do you use one voice or the other in different places and with different audiences?

## Closure

Challenge the class to devise a rule that enables them to convert active to passive sentences. Ask students to present this rule to another class for a test run.

**Focus Activity** # Explanation Signal Words Cloze

The **explanation signal words cloze** activity asks students to fill in a blank with an appropriate signal word.

---

### Objective

This activity helps students identify signal words and practice using them.

---

### Input

Another convention of written explanations is the use of words that signal logical causal links between sequences of events. A cloze activity can help focus students' attention on the use of these words. For this activity, teachers need to copy a well-structured explanation that includes clear signal words such as *because, as a result, consequently,* and so forth. Teachers should list the signal words, together with some options, at the bottom of the page—and add some extras. In one exercise, the explanation might be of an event or process that is familiar to students; in another, the event might be one with which they are not familiar.

---

### Procedure

1. Ask students to work in pairs, small groups, or independently.

2. Present the explanation with its missing words.

3. Tell students to fill in the words.

4. Prompt students to compare their versions with those of others and with the original.

---

### Metacognitive Discussion

Students discuss differences in the sense of the text caused by the use of different signal words, making critical judgments about the appropriateness of the new signal words and those of the original author.

---

### Closure

Change the range of signal words commonly found in explanations.

**Focus Activity**

# Text Reconstruction of an Explanation

In **text reconstruction of an explanation**, students reconstruct a text that has been cut into its logical parts.

## Objective

This activity focuses students on the logical, causal links in explanations and the meaningful links between paragraphs in an explanation.

## Input

The teacher physically cuts up an explanation text into its event sequences, preparing sufficient copies for each working group or individual. Students need to be somewhat familiar with the topic.

## Procedure

1. Ask students to work in pairs, small groups, or independently.

2. Give students a mixed up pile of explanation events and challenge them to put the events back in order.

3. After working for a time, direct students to share their products with another group or student.

4. Share the original text with the students.

5. Lead students to discuss how they were able to figure out the correct order of events and to identify signal words or other logical constructions that aided them. Guide them to also discuss why they got a part out of sequence.

## Metacognitive Discussion

Ask students to think about whether they preferred their versions of the explanation and whether it is desirable to have more than one text explaining the same event or process. (Lead them to think about audience.)

## Closure

Ask groups and individuals to check each other's reconstructions.

**Focus Activity**   # What If . . .

The **what if** . . . activity asks students to pretend that certain things in nature suddenly change and to explain what might happen under these new circumstances.

### Objective

This activity challenges students to compose creative explanations.

### Input

Teachers might use common happenings such as, If a snowman didn't melt . . . , If the sun didn't rise . . . , If a river flowed uphill . . . , and so forth as sentence starters, then challenge students to explain why or how.

### Procedure

1. Offer students a number of starters and challenge them to come up with their own.

2. Organize students into pairs and ask pairs to select one starter and discuss, draw, or image an explanation.

3. Tell pairs to then construct a written explanation jointly.

### Metacognitive Discussion

Ask students to compare their written explanations with myths.

### Closure

Encourage students to read their explanations aloud to a group of four to six others.

SkyLight Training and Publishing Inc.

# WRITING Explanations

CHAPTER 15

## Introduction to the Explanation Writing Model Program

The following thinking and writing explanation focus activities demonstrate how some activities can be brought together in a program that might last several days. The model program for explanations is a unit about burning, aimed at Grades 3 to 6. The context of the study is a science unit. The types of thinking that are targeted are sequencing, inferring, generalizing, composing cause and effect, predicting, evaluating, drawing conclusions, and observing. The thinking frames used in this unit include the event network, explanatory sketch board, and analogy frames. The specific achievement objectives of the program are shown here.

The oral language objectives are to help students

1. organize what they say in a logical sequence;

2. use words that signal the reasons why something happened (causes);

3. listen to speakers and identify how their explanations are structured;

4. take the roles of recorders, reporters, and summarizers during discussion;

5. use the envoy strategy to interact with other groups;

6. elaborate (add detail about) an event mentioned by a previous speaker.

The specific exploring language objectives are to help students

1. explore the language choices made by authors of explanations;

2. identify the common conventions of an explanation, including the use of the present tense and cause-and-effect structures.

The explanation thinking objectives are to help students

1. use an event network, explanatory sketch board, and analogy frame prior to composing oral and written explanations;

2. use an expressive writing technique during science tasks;

3. use directing questions while reading for information.

The science objectives for this unit are to help students

1. understand the meaning of burning, its causes and effects;

2. understand current and historical explanations of burning;

3. observe and sketch examples of burning;

4. investigate why things burn;

5. reconsider their original views about burning.

To prepare for this unit, teachers need to

1. prepare response and completion statements;

2. prepare brainstorm, explanatory sketch board, analogy, and event network thinking frames;

3. prepare Burning Learning Logs for each student. In the front of the logs, the teacher might suggest listing the following:

   • Things I learned about burning today

   • Things about burning that I'm still not sure about

   • Key words from today's burning science lesson

   • Ways in which the teacher could help me learn better

   • Things I could do to help myself learn better

4. collect and display books about burning.

5. prepare model explanation texts, some on transparencies.

The focus activities in this chapter are linked to show a logical progression for the program. Session numbers are used to remind the reader that products from earlier activities may be used again. Most strongly linked activities are those in the sections working with writing frames and thinking frames.

SkyLight Training and Publishing Inc.

# Building Knowledge of the Topic

**Focus Activity**

# Collecting Students' *Before* Views

**Collecting students' *before* views** of burning is an activity that asks students to respond and complete statements about burning. (Session 1)

**Objective**

This activity helps students consider their beliefs about burning before studying about it and enables teachers to assess students' prior knowledge.

**Input**

Teachers need to prepare response and completion statements relevant to the topic either on pages that students can share with another student or as a wall chart. (Statements should be numbered so that pairs can respond to the numbered statements on their answer sheet.) Students require paper strips on which they write their completion statements.

**Procedure**

1. Ask students to work independently or in pairs.

2. Pass out or display one response and completion statement. Prompt students to write Yes or No responses, complete the statements, and write their completion statements on the paper strips. The task may appear as shown in figure 15.1.

---

*Response Statements:*                          *Students' Responses*

  1. Steel will not burn.                    Yes          No

  2. Things need oxygen to burn.       Yes          No

*Completion Statements:*

  3. Things will burn if . . .

  4. Wood produces heat when it burns because . . .

---

*Figure 15.1*

3. Produce a bar graph based on the Yes and No responses and display the paper strips with the completion statements on the wall.

**Metacognitive Discussion**

1. Based on the bar graph, where do we need to focus our research?

2. How might this activity help us read and write to learn?

**Closure**

Challenge the class to design research questions based on the bar graph and to group similar answers to the completion statements in a wall display.

SkyLight Training and Publishing Inc.

**Focus Activity**   # Brainstorm

In the **brainstorm** activity, students prepare the questions about burning that they would like answered during the unit. (Session 2)

---

**Objective**

As a result of this activity, students should be reminded of what they know, organize their known information in a useful format, and design research questions to further their knowledge of the topic.

---

**Input**

The teacher provides strips of paper to record the questions on and a wall display for posting them. Students need to be familiar with what brainstorming means.

---

**Procedure**

1. Invite the class to brainstorm questions about burning and to write them on the paper strips as they are reported.

2. Lead students to group the questions according to topic, label the groups of questions to indicate what they are generally about, and post the questions and labels as a wall display.

3. Encourage students to choose to be in a group that researches answers to a set of related questions.

---

**Metacognitive Discussion**

Reflect with students on the advantage of having research questions that provide a focus for learning, before students read or write.

---

**Closure**

Finalize research groups for a future session and have them think about where they might find the resources that they will use to answer these questions.

**Focus Activity**

# Before Event Network Frame

The **before event network frame** is an activity in which the students and teacher jointly construct the frame to show what the students think might happen when paper burns. (Session 3)

## Objective

As a result of this activity, teachers should have a measure of the beliefs students have about burning.

## Input

Students need some knowledge of the event network frame before attempting this exercise. Although this activity is teacher-directed, students may need large sheets of paper so they can complete the event network as a group.

## Procedure

1. Begin by safely burning a piece of paper and discussing the simple changes of state from solid to gas.

2. Draw two boxes, one containing the word paper, the other the word smoke.

3. Then ask students to think about what the flame and heat might have done to the paper—to form a visual image of this process and to sketch what they see. Encourage students to share and talk about their sketches.

4. Then assign students in groups to complete the event network frame.

5. Now, use an envoy strategy in which one person moves to another group and shares his or her group's completed event network frame.

6. Finally, tell the envoy to return to his or her home group. Challenge the group to compose a summary sentence about burning and write the sentence below their event network.

## Metacognitive Discussion

How did sketching and imaging assist you in completing the event network frame?

## Closure

Encourage students to share their completed frames, then display them.

**Focus Activity** # Summary Discussion

In the **summary discussion**, students discuss what they know about burning and prepare a summary of their state of knowledge. (Session 4)

## Objective

This activity helps students listen and construct a summary of what is known about burning.

## Input

The activity works best as a class and with a competent listener as summarizer and competent writers as recorder and reporter. With classes that do not contain fluent writers, the teacher or adult helpers should take the three roles.

## Procedure

1. Three students (or adult helpers) are chosen to act in the following roles:

    a. Summarizer—whose responsibility is to stop the discussion from time-to-time and provide oral summaries of what has been said so far (Note: Be sure to make these stops every couple of minutes or so);

    b. Recorder—whose duty is to write a précis (or summary) provided by the summarizer;

    c. Reporter—who receives the précis and reads it to the class.

2. Lead the class to discuss burning.

3. Ask the reporter to read the précis to the class.

## Metacognitive Discussion

In what ways were the summaries and précis different from what other students said in class? Why were they different?

## Closure

Encourage students to make a written entry in their personal Burning Learning Logs, noting what they now know about burning.

**Focus Activity** # Expert Views

**Expert views** is an activity that informs students about historical scientific views of the process of burning or combustion. (Session 5)

## Objective

This activity challenges students' beliefs about burning. By the completion of this activity, students should be able to state expert beliefs about burning and identify how these differ from their own beliefs.

## Input

The teacher needs to locate historical accounts of combustion, such as the seventeenth-century belief that fire was one of the four natural elements, as well as seventeenth- and eighteenth-century theories of German scientist Georg Ernst Stahl and of French scientist Antoine Laurent Lavoisier.

## Procedure

1. Read and discuss the historical material with students.

2. Give students a purpose for listening, namely, to identify key vocabulary (e.g., fuel, heat, and oxygen).

3. Model and demonstrate the use of directing questions during the reading. That is, prior to reading a section of text, pose a question that takes most of that section of text to answer. (Note: This is in addition to the task of identifying key vocabulary and should be used two or three times during the session.)

4. Challenge students, working in groups, to compose their best answers to the directing question. Encourage groups to share their answers with the class.

5. Invite student groups to report their best answers to class.

## Metacognitive Discussion

The focus here should be on the kind of directing question that best gives a purpose for listening (or reading). Students should note that questions that take much of the text to answer (fat questions) will serve their purpose better than more focused questions (skinny questions).

## Closure

Ask groups to state one expert idea that surprised or challenged their thinking.

**Focus Activity** # Focus Stage

**Focus stage** is a series of paired science and language activities that explore the concept of burning. (Session 6)

---

### Objective

This activity helps students reconsider or extend their views on burning.

---

### Input

For the science component teachers will need matches, candles, a magnifying glass, paper, a tray of water, and a jar.

For the language component, they will need, prepared on large pieces of paper, event networks, analogies frames, or room for an explanation sketch board. The age and ability of your students will determine how many of these science and language activities they will complete.

---

### Procedure

See figure 15.2 for paired science and language tasks.

---

### Metacognitive Discussion

Ask students to reflect on how (or if) the language activities assisted them to understand the science concepts.

---

### Closure

Challenge the class to make a summary statement about burning that you write down and students copy into their books.

# Science and Language Tasks

| Step | Science | Language |
|------|---------|----------|
| 1. | Light a match. Observe the flame. | Use an event network, analogy frame, or explanation sketch board frame to promote discussion about what burning is. |
| 2. | Bring a live match gradually closer to a lighted candle until it bursts into flame. | Ask groups to observe and discuss this step. Use the envoy strategy to have groups share conclusions. During the discussion, ask one student to take the role of summarizer, who asks the group to stop from time to time and construct an oral summary of the previous speaker(s) explanation. Ask another student to take the role of recorder and another take the role of envoy reporter. |
| 3. | Start a piece of paper burning with a magnifying glass. | Challenge students to act out the process: some acting as the sun's rays, others acting as the magnifying glass, others acting as the fibers that make up the paper. Hot-spot actors, that is—direct students to "freeze" and instruct other class members to ask them questions about their roles. |
| 4. (may complete in a different session) | Place a jar over a burning candle. Place different sized jars over burning candles. Place a candle and a jar in tray of water. Light the candle and cover it with the jar. (What happens to the water level? Why?) | Tell students to use the expressive writing-to-learn approach in the Burning Learning Logs to record each or some of the experiments. Lead students to use event network frames in groups to explain why or how results occurred. |
| 5. | How many examples of burning can we identify? List them. | Ask groups to decide which of the listed items are able to burn and group and label the examples. Direct each group to explain why a particular example is thought to be burnable. Jointly construct an event network frame with the students. |

*Figure 15.2*

# Modeling Explanations

**Focus Activity** ## Model an Explanation

In this activity, the teacher **models an explanation** and an explanation writing frame. (Session 7)

---

**Objective**

This activity challenges students to describe explanation texts modeled by the teacher, to identify these same conventions on an explanation writing frame, to use this frame to think about burning, and to record their beliefs.

---

**Input**

The teacher needs to locate good examples of explanations to read and model to the class. The teacher also needs copies of the explanation writing frames.

---

**Procedure**

1. Read explanations to or along with students (implicit modeling).

2. Read and discuss explanations with students (explicit modeling).

3. Describe how explanation frames mirror the conventions of written explanations, and show students how to use them.

4. Challenge students, working in pairs or individually, to draft explanations in the frame. Collect and grade these explanations before returning them to the students.

---

**Metacognitive Discussion**

Students should reflect on whether the explanation frame assisted them to draft their texts.

---

**Closure**

Invite groups to share their draft explanations.

# Working With Explanation Thinking Frames

**Focus Activity**  ## Introducing Thinking Frames

**Introducing thinking frames** is an activity in which three thinking frames (event network, explanation sketch board, and analogy) are constructed jointly by the teacher and students. (Session 8)

---

### Objective

The activity provides students with ways of thinking about burning prior to writing.

---

### Input

The teacher needs to have display copies of each frame, and have one of each available to complete with the students. The teacher will also need a safe facility to demonstrate how paper burns. Finally, the teacher will need white posterboard or large sheets of paper for modeling a think-aloud protocol while writing expressively.

---

### Procedure

1. Work with the class to jointly construct an event network frame that represents how and why paper burns.

2. Lead the class to jointly construct a sketch board frame that illustrates what might be happening inside a flame.

3. Guide the class to jointly construct an analogy frame, creating analogies that explain burning.

4. Model an expressive writing-to-learn technique—pause during discussion and experiments to allow students to write expressively. (Students should record their personal, immediate thoughts, feelings, and observations that help them explain why or how something happens.)

---

### Metacognitive Discussion

Students should be prompted to appreciate that they can write to learn as well as write to record.

---

### Closure

Link this exercise to instruction on what to put in the Burning Learning Log.

# Working With Explanation Writing Frames

**Focus Activity**    # Writing Independently

**Writing independently** gives students an opportunity to prepare a written explanation of burning. (Session 9)

### Objective

This activity allows teachers to assess students' ability to write explanations and to assess their ability to translate knowledge into written explanation.

### Input

Students must have some knowledge of burning in order to prepare an explanation and need to be reminded of the thinking frames and writing frames that might assist them in this activity. (Note: These should be already displayed around the classroom.)

### Procedure

1. Before writing, ask students to identify their audience and purpose for preparing the explanation. They should discuss who will read the explanation, how this will affect the way it is written, and the purpose of explanation texts.

2. Tell students to write an explanation using the explanation writing frame. (Later you may challenge students to compose fictional explanations in the form of myths.)

3. Encourage students to confer in pairs and/or in groups about their written explanations, in order to anchor their learning to ideas consistent with those currently accepted by scientists.

4. Direct students to share and discuss their explanations with a partner. In addition to responding to written explanations, you might encourage pairs to investigate fire-proofing of material or how fire extinguishers work.

### Metacognitive Discussion

The class discusses how using thinking frames and writing frames has assisted them in the process of learning.

**Closure**

Assess and lead students to assess their written explanation texts and their knowledge of burning, doing the following tasks:

*Science Tasks*

1. Summarize what has been learned about burning.

2. Determine what can be added to the brainstorm frame.

3. Decide if the response and completion statements need to be changed.

4. Take a multiple-choice test on burning.

5. Assess the Burning Learning Logs.

*Thinking and Language Tasks*

6. Summarize what has been learned about writing explanations.

7. Determine how using explanation thinking frames aided the process of writing explanations.

8. Identify conventional structures in the students' explanations.

9. Review what was learned about thinking prior to writing.

# Catch Them
# Thinking and Writing
# Arguments and Discussions

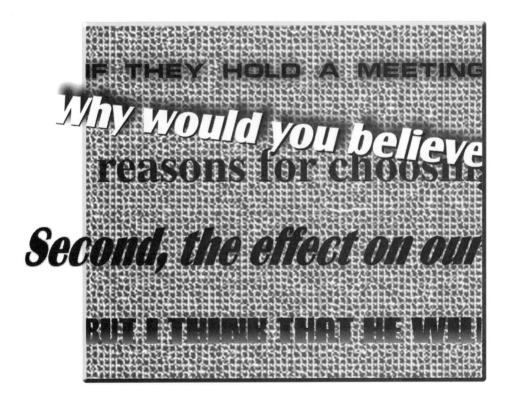

# Overview of Thinking and Writing Arguments and Discussions

## Arguments and discussions are

Your opinion

In the present tense

Supported by reason and research

## Writing arguments and discussions means using

Argument and Discussion Writing Frames

## Thinking arguments and discussions means using the

Discussion Web Frames

Perspective Frames

Socratic Questions Frames

Creative Problem-Solving Frames

SCAMPER Problem-solving Frames

## Arguments and discussion thinking involves

| Analyzing | Evaluating |
| --- | --- |
| Composing bias | Making decisions |
| Composing assumptions | Solving problems |
| Linking | Summarizing |
| Drawing conclusions | Questioning |
| Combining ideas | Predicting counterarguments |
| Ordering | Considering multiple perspectives |

## Types of arguments and discussions include

Event

Object

Idea

*Figure Part 6.1*

SkyLight Training and Publishing Inc.

# WHAT ARE Arguments and Discussions?

CHAPTER 16

These types of factual texts state either one side (argument) or both sides (discussion) of an issue. Following are examples:

- When we protest that the school cafeteria food is bad and nothing but bad, we are composing an argument.

- When we write about Democratic and Republican platforms on the same issue, we are usually writing a discussion.

Arguments and discussions are even found inside other types of writing. For example, in a description about your pet tarantula, you might argue that tarantulas make good pets. Mixing different types of writing can add interest.

Although there are object, event, and idea arguments and discussions that serve a wide range of purposes, they are still an easy text type to spot.

- All arguments and discussions are factual to the extent that they are supported by objective evidence.

- Most often, arguments and discussions are written in the present tense (although those about historic events might use the past tense).

- Many use separate paragraphs for each new argument or counterargument.

- Often, there are links between these arguments so that the whole text hangs together.

- Writers may signal new arguments with The next reason . . . , Another reason . . . , Some people might say. . . .

# Why Think and Write Arguments and Discussions?

We probably do not naturally talk and write arguments and discussions in any formal manner. But clearly, we can and do argue from an early age! Written arguments and discussions are a bit unfriendly but, unlike other factual text types in this book, they do allow us to record particular understandings.

Written arguments and discussions are less common in lower grades in which narratives, observations, and descriptions are the norm. Perhaps this is because arguments and discussions require writers to make a transition from writing about things to writing about ideas. Students must move their thinking from specific instances (why I should have a dog) to the general or generic (why everyone should be allowed to keep dogs). However, students should never be dissuaded from attempting all types of writing—even Grade 1 students may write arguments and discussions in just a few words!

# What Do Arguments and Discussions Look and Sound Like?

There are different types of arguments and discussions, as follows, which share common characteristics:

- Event arguments and discussions (for example, whether atmospheric nuclear testing is good or bad)
- Object arguments and discussions (for example, whether the World Wide Web should be censored)
- Idea arguments and discussions (for example, whether the beliefs of a particular religion are right or wrong)

The argument and discussion, modeled in figures 16.1 and 16.2, include some techniques of writing that are designed to convince readers. These persuasive writing techniques include exaggeration, repetition, and the use of emotive language and imagery. The model argument shown in figure 16.1 uses techniques to engage the reader by getting right up their noses, literally. For example, a sensory image, exaggeration, and the sounds of language are effectively used in the line People die because they drive. This restatement leaves the reader in no doubt as to the argument.

# Model Argument

## Ban the Automobile

### Background (why you are writing this argument)

Do you like the smell of car exhaust? Millions of cars are polluting our cities, and people are saying we need to solve the problems cars create.

### Thesis (the argument)

To solve this problem, I believe people should be banned from owning automobiles. I believe this for safety, economic, and environmental reasons.

### First Reason

First, cars are not safe. This weekend five people were slaughtered on our roads, not to mention the countless number of people maimed in nonfatal accidents. People die because they drive.

### Second Reason and Alternative

Cars should be banned because they cost too much. Money spent buying cars would be better spent on schools and hospitals. In addition, buying gas for a car costs a lot of money. Going by bus may not be as convenient, but it is cheap.

### Third Reason and Alternative

Cars should be banned for environmental reasons. Buses running on compressed natural gas (CNG) give off less pollution. In fact, one CNG bus gives off less pollution than one gas-fueled car and can carry fifty people.

### Counterargument

Some people might argue that people need cars. Okay, some people might need a car from time to time, but many more people could and should walk to work, and many others could and should take the bus.

### Restatement

We do not need cars. It makes sense on safety, environmental, and economic grounds to ban cars from our roads.

*Figure 16.1*

SkyLight Training and Publishing Inc.

# Model Discussion
## Should We Ban the Automobile?

## Thesis

There are reasons for and against banning ownership of automobiles.

## Discussion Topic One

First, it might be argued that cars are not safe. But, if we were to ban something because people might die doing it, we would have to stop using all other forms of transportation. There is risk in everything.

## Discussion Topic Two

Others might say that we should ban cars because they are too expensive to buy and run; money should be spent on more important things like better schools and hospitals. But this takes away individuals' freedom to use hard-earned money the way they want to. If they can afford to run a car, why should they be forced into a bus?

## Discussion Topic Three

The answer to that, some people would say, is that cars should be banned for environmental reasons. One bus running on CNG and carrying fifty people pollutes less than one gas-fueled car carrying at the most six people. But, new cars running on unleaded fuel are less of an environmental hazard, some people need cars because it is too far to walk to work and school, and buses are sometimes unavailable.

## Conclusion

There are good reasons on both sides. Perhaps if we thought more about each other and the planet we share, we might use our cars less and we might all benefit in the end.

*Figure 16.2*

# How Do We Start Thinking and Writing Arguments and Discussions?

## What Are Argument and Discussion Writing Frames?

As we have seen when looking at other writing frames, these are structures for holding something in a predetermined shape. The graded argument and discussion writing frames (figs. 16.3–16.8) in this chapter gradually introduce students to the complexities of drafting this text type. Again, the shape is signaled by subheadings that prompt students to think about the conventions of this type of writing. The most basic argument (fig. 16.3) and discussion (fig. 16.6) frames prompt students to write

- a thesis (that says what they are arguing or discussing)
- a body (where the arguments are outlined)
- a restatement or conclusion (of the thesis)

The expanded frames (figs. 16.4 and 16.7) prompt students to write

- a background statement (what lead up to this argument)
- a thesis (that says what they are arguing or discussing)
- a body (where the arguments are outlined)
- a restatement or conclusion (of the thesis)

The counterargument frame (fig. 16.5) and the discussion background frame (fig. 16.8) prompt writers to add to the body of their argument or discussion and write

- a background statement (what lead up to this argument)
- a thesis (that says what they are arguing or discussing)
- a body (where the arguments are outlined, and where counter-arguments are stated)
- a restatement or conclusion (of the thesis).

### Using the Argument and Discussion Writing Frames

Argument and discussion writing frames are used by students who are unfamiliar with these text types. The frames act like coat hooks on which learners can hang their ideas. The resultant text is likely to be well-structured, but devoid of authenticity, style, and a writer's voice. These characteristics of good writing tend to emerge when students revise, edit, confer with, and act on another student's response to their writing.

# Argument Writing Frame: Basic

The title of my argument is _____

## Thesis

Write a paragraph that says what you are arguing for or against.

*I believe that . . .*

_____

_____

_____

*I believe this because . . .*

_____

_____

_____

## Body

Write paragraphs that say why you believe this.

*First, I believe this because . . .*

_____

_____

_____

*The second reason is . . .*

_____

_____

_____

*Finally, I think that . . .*

_____

_____

_____

## Restatement

Write a paragraph that says again what you are arguing for or against.

*For these reasons, I believe that . . .*

_____

_____

_____

*Figure 16.3*

SkyLight Training and Publishing Inc.

# Argument Writing Frame: Expanded

The title of my argument is _____

## Background

Write a paragraph that says something about the issue and why people might have different points of view about it.

_____

_____

## Thesis

Write a paragraph saying what you are arguing for or against.

*I believe that . . .*

_____

_____

*I believe this because . . .*

_____

_____

## Body

Write paragraphs saying why you believe this.

*First, I believe this because . . .*

_____

_____

_____

*The second reason/another reason/a final reason is . . .*

_____

_____

_____

## Restatement

Write a paragraph that says again what you believe.

*For these reasons, I believe that . . .*

_____

_____

_____

*Figure 16.4*

# Argument Writing Frame: Counterargument

The title of my argument is _____

## Background

Write a paragraph that says something about the issue and why people might have different points of view about it.

_____

## Thesis

Write paragraphs that state what you are arguing for or against.

*I believe that . . .*

_____

*I believe this because . . .*

_____

## Body

Write paragraphs that state why you believe this.

*First, I believe this because . . .*

_____

*The second reason is . . .*

_____

*Another reason I believe that . . .*

_____

*Finally, I think that . . .*

_____

## Counterargument

Write an opposite view, then say what is wrong with this view.

*Some people might say that . . ., but*

_____

## Restatement

Write a paragraph that states again what you believe.

*For these reasons, I believe that . . .*

_____

*Figure 16.5*

SkyLight Training and Publishing Inc.

# Discussion Writing Frame: Basic

The title of my discussion is _____

## Thesis

Write paragraphs saying what people are arguing for and against.

*Some people believe that . . .*

_____

_____

*On the other hand, other people believe that . . .*

_____

_____

## Body

Write paragraphs that give both sides of the argument.

*First, some people believe that . . .*

_____

_____

*A second argument put forward by some people is that . . .*

_____

_____

*People opposed to that view say that . . .*

_____

_____

## Conclusion

Write a paragraph that shows you have thought about both sides. You might decide who has the stronger case, but you might like to just provide a brief summary of the main points stated by each side.

_____

_____

_____

_____

*Figure 16.6*

# Discussion Writing Frame: Expanded

The title of my discussion is _____

## Thesis

Write paragraphs saying what people are arguing for and against.

*Some people believe that . . .*

_____

*On the other hand, other people believe that . . .*

_____

## Body

Write paragraphs that give both sides of the argument.

*First, some people believe that . . .*

_____

*On the other hand, others say that . . .*

_____

*A second argument put forward by some people is that . . .*

_____

*People opposed to that view say that . . .*

_____

*Most people agree that . . .*

_____

*But there are still some people who suggest that . . .*

_____

## Conclusion

Write a paragraph that shows you have thought about both sides. You might decide who has the stronger case, but you might just provide a brief summary of the main points stated by each side.

_____

_____

_____

_____

*Figure 16.7*

# Discussion Writing Frame: Background

The title of my discussion is _____

## Background

Write a paragraph that states something about the issue and why people might have different points of view about it.

_____

_____

## Thesis

Write paragraphs stating what people are arguing for and against.

*Some people believe that . . .*

_____

*On the other hand, other people believe that . . .*

_____

## Body

Write paragraphs in the body that give both sides of the argument.

*First, some people believe that . . .*

_____

*On the other hand, others say that . . .*

_____

*A second argument put forward by some people is that . . .*

_____

*Most people agree that . . .*

_____

*But there are still some people who suggest that . . .*

_____

## Conclusion

Write a paragraph that shows you have thought about both sides. You might decide who has the stronger case, but you might just provide a brief summary of the main points stated by each side.

_____

_____

*Figure 16.8*

*How to Introduce Argument and Discussion Writing Frames*

The explicit modeling of argument and discussion writing frames should be conducted along with a program of implicit modeling. Teachers should read arguments and discussions aloud to and along with their classes, and students should have opportunities to read these text types recreationally.

Clearly, it is easier for students to begin with the basic writing frames for arguments and discussions before moving on to the more complex argument and discussion writing frames. For example, to make the task of writing an argument easier, Grade 1 and 2 students might not write a background to their argument but just state their position and continue from there. These same students might find it a bit too difficult to prepare a counterargument. These features, which appear in the frames, might be deleted for lower-grade or beginning writers. Similar alterations might be made in the discussion frames to aid beginners in concentrating on the basics.

## Assessing and Reflecting on Argument and Discussion Writing Frames

A rubric is shown in figure 16.9 and is designed to assist teachers and students in assessing progress in writing arguments and discussions. The rubric supports a formative assessment approach, rather than summative assessment. It uses the approach of representing progress on a continuum from dependent to independent language behavior and performance. Teachers may find it useful to date a rating placed on the rubric.

## What Are Argument and Discussion Thinking Frames?

The purpose of an argument or discussion thinking frame is to help students prepare to talk or write these text types. These frames engage students in argument and discussion thinking, which contrasts with the kind of thinking required to compose, for example, a procedure. The following thinking frames are designed to help students record and manipulate information in clever ways prior to crafting an argument or discussion. Again, these frames might be used for teaching, that is, the teacher uses them with students to help them think arguments and discussions. But later they should become learning frames as students use them independently. The following argument and discussion thinking frames are described:

- Discussion web frames
- Perspective frame
- The Socratic questions frame
- SCAMPER problem-solving frame

SkyLight Training and Publishing Inc.

# Assessing Argument and Discussion Writing

|                                                                   | Dependent | Independent |
|-------------------------------------------------------------------|:---------:|:-----------:|
| Decides on purpose                                                | ←———————————————→ | |
| Determines audience                                               | ←———————————————→ | |
| **Argument and Discussion Writing Frames**                        |           |             |
| Employs joint construction                                        | ←———————————————→ | |
| Uses independent construction                                     | ←———————————————→ | |
| **Meaning**                                                       |           |             |
| Provides enough information                                       | ←———————————————→ | |
| Expresses ideas clearly                                           | ←———————————————→ | |
| Keeps to topic                                                    | ←———————————————→ | |
| Has voice                                                         | ←———————————————→ | |
| Achieves purpose                                                  | ←———————————————→ | |
| **Structure**                                                     |           |             |
| General characteristics of arguments and discussions             | ←———————————————→ | |
| Background                                                        | ←———————————————→ | |
| Thesis                                                            | ←———————————————→ | |
| Reasons                                                           | ←———————————————→ | |
| Alternatives                                                      | ←———————————————→ | |
| Counterarguments                                                  | ←———————————————→ | |
| Restatement                                                       | ←———————————————→ | |
| Conclusion                                                        | ←———————————————→ | |
| Exaggeration                                                      | ←———————————————→ | |
| Repetition                                                        | ←———————————————→ | |
| Emotive language                                                  | ←———————————————→ | |
| Imagery                                                           | ←———————————————→ | |

| | Yes | No |
|---|:---:|:---:|
| Includes other text types in argument or discussion | Yes | No |
| Needs argument/discussion writing frames | Yes | No |

*Figure 16.9*

*Using Discussion Web Frames*

Discussion web frames can be used to think about issues prior to writing arguments and discussions. Essentially, they assist students to generate, record, and evaluate ideas. Students begin by clearly establishing the issue (fig. 16.10), the problem (fig. 16.11), or the theory (fig. 16.12) that they wish to think about. These are written in the space provided at the top of the discussion web frame.

When using the discussion web frame (fig. 16.10), issues for consideration might stem from literature. For example, after reading the tale of Little Red Riding Hood, readers might take the view that the wolf was bad. Alternatively, the issue may stem from history. For example, after reading about the potato famine in Ireland, readers might conclude that Britain was to blame for the potato famine.

A problem statement might stem from a social studies program, for example Should we try to reduce smog levels over our big cities? In this case, students list reasons for and against reducing smog and then decide on a conclusion (see fig. 16.11). It might be very useful for students to complete a PMI chart for each alternative, listing P (positive) features, M (minus or negative) features, and I (interesting) unexpected outcomes of adopting a particular alternative. Using the PMI chart ensures that each choice is evaluated using the same criteria.

Discussion web frames can be used to evaluate theories (fig. 16.12). For example, in a science class, students might come up with two plausible explanations for the depletion of certain type of fish and need to list their evidence for each hypothesis before reaching a best guess. In each case, students should be involved in research prior to and while using the discussion web frame.

Students may question the need to complete both sides of a discussion web frame prior to writing arguments or discussions. Therefore, the

---

# Discussion Web Frame 1

Write a sentence that says what issue you want to think about.

_____

Reasons Yes                                    Reasons No

_____                _____
_____                _____
_____                _____

**Conclusion**

_____
_____

*Figure 16.10*

# Discussion Web Frame 2

Write a sentence that says what problem you want to think about.

_____

Solution One                             Solution Two

_____      _____

_____      _____

_____      _____

**Our Best Solutions**

_____

_____

*Figure 16.11*

# Discussion Web Frame 3

Write a sentence that says what theory you want to think about.

_____

Theory One                              Theory Two

_____      _____

_____      _____

_____      _____

**Our Best Guess**

_____

_____

*Figure 16.12*

teacher will have to point out that completing the frame will help them choose the strongest side when writing an argument or the strongest points when writing a discussion. Further, when students use the problem argument writing frame, they need to understand both sides of an argument so that they can compose counterarguments, usually by focusing on the weakest argument from the opposing side.

Again, the teacher will need to make sure students have sufficiently researched the topic before using the writing frames. Also, students will require the teacher's assistance in composing their statements because these statements give a purpose for listening, reading, and viewing. The best method is for students to complete discussion webs jointly, then share them with the class before they jointly or independently construct argument or discussion texts.

## *Using Perspective Frames*

Perspective frames (fig. 16.13) lead students to think in six complex ways. They provide a means of thinking through events, ideas, or issues prior to writing an argument or discussion.

Apart from the talk perspective, these frames are perhaps best suited to students in Grades 3 and above. Even at this level, when used as a prewriting frame, they should be introduced one at a time over several weeks. However, this does not prevent teachers from using the perspectives during class discussion to raise the level of thinking.

Each perspective serves a different purpose, so that perspectives should be carefully selected in the light of the event, idea, or issue under consideration. For example, the talk perspective invites students to talk about something from the point of view of animate and inanimate objects. For example, when thinking about a train crash, students might talk from the point of view of the engineer, passengers, the train itself, the owner of the railroad, and even that of the rails that were perhaps bent as a result of an earthquake. The talk perspective is appropriate when several people and/or objects are involved in the idea, event, or object to be discussed.

Alternatively, the size perspective might lead students to consider the consequence of something. For example, they might consider the consequences of a fight between two people spreading into a community and, eventually escalating into a war. The space/location perspective may lead students to reconsider the horror of war. For example, if that war were being waged over their backyard fence and not on the other side of the world. Again, the object, event, or idea to be considered determines what perspective is chosen.

The culture perspective helps students appreciate the ways different societies might view the same object or event. For example, most Japanese have no problem with hunting whales while other cultures have banned the practice.

Looking at any object or event from different angles provides students with multiple perspectives. For example, looking at a whale from above provides one perspective, but the observer is hardly likely to appreciate the enormous mouth unless he or she sees the open-mouthed whale from the front. Likewise, if, like the blind men in the famous tale, the viewer examines only one part of an elephant, he or she might never comprehend the complete picture.

Time changes the way people think about things. What was okay years ago, like the killing of harp seals off the Pacific coast of the United States, might be frowned on today. But, in the future, as colonies of harp seals grow and fish populations are depleted, people might revert to thinking it okay to kill harp seals. In this example, size and time perspectives overlap.

Each conclusion sentence is designed to motivate students' consideration of an immediate event, idea, or issue to some general level that

# Perspective Frame

Topic: _____

**Time**

What do we think about it now? What will we think about it later? What did people think about it before?

_____

*Conclusion Sentence*

_____

**Size**

If it got much bigger or smaller, would that change the way we think about it?

_____

*Conclusion Sentence*

_____

**Space/Location**

What would it look like close-up? or from a distance?

_____

*Conclusion Sentence*

_____

**Culture**

What would the first settlers in our country think about it? What would visitors from another country think about it?

_____

*Conclusion Sentence*

_____

**Talk**

If people and objects could talk, what might they say?

_____

*Conclusion Sentence*

_____

**Angle**

What does it look like from above? the side? from below?

_____

*Conclusion Sentence*

_____

*Figure 16.13*

says something about us as humans. Conclusion sentences should be written jointly by a group of students after talking about a particular perspective. For example, discussion using the talk perspective may result in students concluding that we need to appreciate other people's points of view. The space/location perspective may lead students to conclude that distance dulls our appreciation of events.

In short, the perspective frame, modeled in figure 16.14, provides ways of thinking through events, ideas, and issues prior to writing and a way of reaching some big generalizations about the human condition.

## Using the Socratic Questions Frame

Socratic questions (Paul 1991) are designed to promote the kind of critical thinking required to write arguments and discussions. The frame helps students evaluate their thinking, compare it with that of other students in a group, and consider multiple ideas and links between and among ideas.

Before using the Socratic questions frame (fig. 16.15), students must design a debatable statement, such as Whaling should be banned. Then they ask four questions in turn to discuss the debatable statement.

Question One: What evidence leads you to think this way, to hold a particular view? Students consider the source of their evidence and associated belief.

Question Two: Is there additional evidence for my view? Students seek further evidence supporting their view and should be encouraged to provide reasons why they hold a particular view.

Question Three: What would someone who disagrees with you say? Students consider the views of people who hold opposite or conflicting perspectives. This perspective helps students appreciate other points of view.

Question Four: What are the consequences of holding this position? Students consider the repercussions of holding a particular opinion—either in support or opposition to the statement.

As modeled in figure 16.16, groups write the debatable statement under the heading What we believe and discuss the debatable statement using each question in turn. Recorders take notes that are shared with the class and the notes are used as the basis for the joint or independent construction of an argument or discussion text.

SkyLight Training and Publishing Inc.

# Model Perspective Frame

## Topic: Whaling Should Be Banned

**TIME PERSPECTIVE:** What do we think about whaling now? What will we think about whaling later? What did people think about whaling before?

Most people would agree because many whale species are near extinction. As long as numbers are low they will continue to support the ban. Some people would say it's wrong to kill such a magnificent animal like the blue whale. In early days when whales were thought to be plentiful and there was a demand for whale products, few people minded about killing whales.

**Conclusion Sentence:** Time and the threat of extinction change our view of events.

**SIZE PERSPECTIVE:** If whales got much bigger or smaller, would that change the way we think about them?

The blue whale is the biggest animal on earth and because it's so big some people think it should be always protected. It's harder to kill a big animal and that upsets some people. If whales were small, like the size of a sardine, they would be less obvious and probably people wouldn't care so much about people hunting them.

**Conclusion Sentence:** We care more about big animals because they can be easily seen and because they are hard to kill quickly.

**SPACE/LOCATION PERSPECTIVE:** What would whaling look like close-up? from a distance?

Watching a harpoon going into a whale up close and having your face splattered with blood would be horrific. If whales are being hunted a long way away and I can't see it happening I'm not so upset.

**Conclusion Sentence:** Distance dulls your senses about any event.

**CULTURE PERSPECTIVE:** What would the first settlers think about whaling? What would visitors from another country think about whaling?

People from Japan, Norway, Iceland, and Tonga would have no problems with hunting whales. Some indigenous people like the Intuits think it's okay and part of their rights. Other cultures disagree and substitute whale meat with other forms of meat.

**Conclusion Sentence:** Different cultures have their own (valid) points of view.

**TALK PERSPECTIVE:** If whales could talk, what might they say?

The whales wouldn't be happy, but the owners of the whale boat would see hunting as a vital return on investment. The Japanese sushi bar operator wouldn't be happy if we stopped hunting whales, but Greenpeace would be.

**Conclusion Sentence:** It depends on whom you talk to as to what view you get.

**ANGLE PERSPECTIVE:** What does whaling look like from above? the side? from below?

If you were below the whale when the harpoon entered, you would see the whale arch and writhe. From above you would see a widening stain of blood in the water.

**Conclusion Sentence:** What ever angle you look at it, hunting whales is a bloody occupation.

*Figure 16.14*

SkyLight Training and Publishing Inc.

# Socratic Questions Frame

What we believe _____

## Question One

What evidence leads you to think this way, to hold a particular view? (Reflect on why you believe this to be true. Have you always thought this to be true?)

_____
_____
_____
_____

## Question Two

Is there additional evidence for my view? (Consider other people's support for what you believe.)

_____
_____
_____
_____

## Question Three

What would someone who disagrees with you say? (What would people with the opposite belief say?)

_____
_____
_____
_____

## Question Four

What are the consequences of holding this position? (What might happen if you continue to hold this belief? What should/could you do?)

_____
_____
_____
_____

*Figure 16.15*

SkyLight Training and Publishing Inc.

# Model Socratic Questions Frame

What we believe: *We believe that China should stop testing atomic bombs in the atmosphere.*

## Question One

What evidence leads you to think this way, to hold a particular view? (Reflect on why you believe this to be true. Have you always thought this to be true?)

I thought it was okay for the United States and Britain to test their atomic bombs in the atmosphere because they were trying to end a war. But now we should be working toward peace without the threat of killing every person on earth. People get radiation sickness from bombs.

## Question Two

Is there additional evidence for my view? (Consider other people's support for what you believe.)

Other countries don't need to test their bombs in the air—France does it underground and the United States uses computer simulation. Scientists have discovered that aboriginal people from Australia and other people from the Pacific that lived near testing sites have gotten sick. Many groups like the Campaign for Nuclear Disarmament (CND) and Greenpeace want to put an end to testing and world leaders also want to stop the testing.

## Question Three

What would someone who disagrees with you say? (What would people with the opposite belief say?)

Clearly the Chinese don't agree. They say that they need the bomb for defense and that they do not have the money or technology to test underground or in computer simulations.

## Question Four

What are the consequences of holding this position? (What might happen if you continue to hold this belief? What should/could you do?)

I still hold to the view that China should stop testing atomic bombs in the atmosphere. I'm going to write a letter to the Chinese government asking that the testing be stopped.

*Figure 16.16*

## *Using the SCAMPER Problem-Solving Frame*

The SCAMPER problem solving frame (Eberle 1996; see fig. 16.17) can be used by students prior to writing arguments or discussions because it provides them with six ways of solving problems and thinking about issues. Students clearly define the problem or issue. For example, Lead should be excluded from gas because lead-filled exhaust causes brain damage. In groups, students will need to research as they use each of the SCAMPER ways of thinking about the problem.

**S**ubstitute: What could you use or do instead? The substitute way of problem solving may lead to considering research into aromatics as substitutes for lead, or into the use of carpooling as a way of reducing exhaust emissions.

**C**ombine: What could be brought together to solve the problem? The combine way of thinking may lead students to think about how chemists, neurologists, and mechanics might assist in solving the problem.

**A**dapt: What could be changed to solve the problem? The adapt way of thinking may lead students to consider adaptations that would assist in alleviating the problem.

**M**odify: What would happen if we made something larger, greater, stronger, smaller, lighter, or slower? The modify way of thinking may lead students to think of alternate energy sources and the consequences of smog caused by automobile exhaust emissions.

**P**ut to other use: In what other ways or contexts could this problem be viewed or used?

**E**liminate: What could we do without it? The eliminate way of thinking might lead students to consider the positive benefits of reducing lead levels in the atmosphere.

**R**everse: What would you have if you reversed it, turned it around, or changed the parts or order? Reversing the problem as a way of thinking would result in students considering the repercussions of not solving the problem, such as creating more brain damage from lead poisoning.

The SCAMPER way of problem solving is likely to benefit students when writing any text that uses a problem-solution text structure. For example, a report about whales may address the problem of over-hunting and suggest possible solutions. An explanation of why the ozone layer is depleting may lead to a description of what causes the problem and ways of halting the depletion. Arguments and discussions often address problems, including solutions strengthens these texts.

# SCAMPER Problem-Solving Frame

The problem or issue is _____

**S**ubstitute     What could you use instead? What could you do instead?

_____

_____

**C**ombine     What could be brought together to solve the problem?

_____

_____

**A**dapt     What could be changed to solve the problem?

_____

_____

**M**odify     What would happen if we made something larger, greater, stronger, smaller, lighter, or slower?

_____

_____

**P**ut to other use     In what other ways or contexts could this problem be viewed or used?

_____

_____

**E**liminate     What could we do without it?

_____

_____

**R**everse     What would you have if you reversed it, turned it around, or changed the parts or order?

_____

_____

*Figure 16.17*     SCAMPER model reprinted with permission from *SCAMPER: Creative Games and Activities for Imagination Development,* B. Eberle, 1996

*Using the Creative Problem-Solving Frame*

The creative problem-solving (CPS) frame assists students to generate and evaluate solutions to problems faced by fictional and historical characters. For example, as the model CPS (fig. 16.18) illustrates, students might generate creative solutions to a fictional character's problems. Equally, they might generate solutions related to a nation's financial, environmental, or racial problems.

The first step in using a creative problem-solving frame (fig. 16.19) is to determine a problem central to a text or topic of study. This is easy with narratives because they have (essentially) a problem-solution structure (the main character has a problem that they seek to resolve). It is also easy with most historical events. With a little imagination, many other situations can be seen in a problem-solution light, such as animals seeking food and protection and unstable chemicals seeking to combine with other chemicals.

When reading aloud with students or when they are involved in independent reading, teachers might provide students with a purpose for reading by stating the main problem in the form of a question (see fig. 16.18).

When using this frame, students list all their solutions to the problem across the top, then list the evaluation points down the left side. Sometimes an evaluation scale is useful (see the rating code in fig. 16.18).

In the Little Red Riding Hood example, the solution of putting out food has, as one advantage, that the wolf's life would be spared while the solution of killing the wolf would be cheap. When each solution has been evaluated and recorded, students use the rating scale to record their evaluation in the grid. For example, putting out food would save the wolf's life but, in the long run, it would not be cheap. Note that at least one evaluation is listed for each solution.

Again, students might complete the frame in groups, then discuss their thinking with other groups. Solutions might be ranked from excellent to failure and form the basis for discussion and the writing of a factual text.

## Assessing and Reflecting on Argument and Discussion Thinking Frames

To assist teachers in monitoring and recording student progress in using argument and discussion thinking frames, an assessment rubric is provided (fig. 16.20). It is intended to be used for formative assessment, using a continuum from dependent to independent to reflect the degree of accomplishment that a student has achieved at the time of assessment. Teachers are encouraged to share their assessments with students and students are encouraged to use the rubric to assess themselves.

SkyLight Training and Publishing Inc.

# Model Creative Problem-Solving Frame

**Problem**

In the story of Little Red Riding Hood, how might we stop the wolf from attacking Grandmother?

| Ideas / Evaluation of Ideas | Put Out Food | Kill the Wolf | Capture the Wolf | Secure Granny's House |
|---|---|---|---|---|
| Save life | A | C | A | A |
| Is cheap | D | A | B | C |
| Quick solution | F | A | C | C |
| Still a problem | D | A | D | B |
| Most humane | A | F | B | A |

**Our Best Solution**

Although some in our group thought it was not right (humane) to shoot the wolf, this turned out to be our best solution. Many thought that capturing the wolf was a kind solution but you would still have the problem of feeding it, although later we thought that the wolf could be released somewhere else.

**Rating Code:**   A = Excellent idea; B = Very good idea; C = Average idea; D = Below average idea; F = Total failure

*Figure 16.18*

# Creative Problem-Solving Frame

**Problem**

_____

| Ideas / Evaluation of Ideas | | | | |
|---|---|---|---|---|
| | | | | |
| | | | | |
| | | | | |
| | | | | |
| | | | | |

**Our Best Solution**

_____

**Rating Code:**   A = Excellent idea; B = Very good idea; C = Average idea; D = Below average idea; F = Total failure

*Figure 16.19*

# Assessing Argument and Discussion Thinking

|  | Dependent | Independent |
|---|---|---|

**Discussion Web Frames**

Designs statement ←——————————————→

Issue web ←——————————————→

Problem web ←——————————————→

Theory web ←——————————————→

Uses in writing ←——————————————→

**Creative Problem-Solving Frame**

Completes prepared grid ←——————————————→

Completes partial grid ←——————————————→

Designs own grid ←——————————————→

Writes summaries ←——————————————→

**Perspective Frame**

Group frame completed ←——————————————→

Framer used when writing ←——————————————→

Time ←——————————————→

Size ←——————————————→

Space/location ←——————————————→

Culture ←——————————————→

Talk ←——————————————→

Angle ←——————————————→

**Socratic Questions Frame**

Question 1 ←——————————————→

Question 2 ←——————————————→

Question 3 ←——————————————→

Question 4 ←——————————————→

*Figure 16.20*

SkyLight Training and Publishing Inc.

# PRACTICE ACTIVITIES
## to Support Thinking and Writing Arguments and Discussions

CHAPTER 17

## Oral Language Activities

The aim of oral language activities is to support argument and discussion writing, to help students make information about the topic their own, and to practice using the present tense, typical of argument or discussion texts. Note that oral language activities help learners practice using the rhetoric of arguments and discussions, including the use of exaggeration, repetition, and metaphor.

**Focus Activity**

# Ranking

**Ranking** is an activity that encourages students to order something according to some criteria. A simple version of ranking has students select adjectives that describe a fictional or historical character, then rank them from best to least satisfactory descriptor. The same ranking procedure can be used with a list of arguments prior to writing so that the strongest arguments are selected.

### Objective

This activity teaches students how to rank items or ideas and demonstrates the benefits of ranking.

### Input

This activity is best played after using a challenge activity that generates several adjectives written on small cards. If it is not used following challenge, the teacher must lead the class to generate a list of adjectives, verbs, or adverbs before the ranking can commence.

## Procedure

1. Arrange students in groups of three to five members.

2. If played by following challenge, give each group all the word cards for one character, person, or animal. If the activity is done as a stand-alone activity, lead the class to generate words and list the words on small cards before the game commences.

3. Allow groups to spend about ten minutes ranking the cards and justifying their rank order. Emphasize that group consensus on the word ranking is essential.

## Metacognitive Discussion

Students should be challenged to state where the information came from to justify their ranking (e.g., a book or their own value system).

## Closure

Challenge students to share and defend their word rankings with the class.

**Focus Activity**

# Piranha Pool

**Piranha pool** is an activity that allows students to practice debating sides of a discussion. This is a great activity for developing oral and written arguments.

---

**Objective**

This activity develops students' debating skills and allows them to apply argument and discussion techniques.

---

**Input**

Students have researched the same topic and hold opposite views about a debatable aspect of the topic. For example, after reading the tale of Little Red Riding Hood, one student may decide that the wolf was most to blame for what happened to Grandma, whereas another might have decided that Little Red Riding Hood's parents were most to blame. (Note: The teacher might choose an historical topic.)

---

**Procedure**

1. Establish two student groups, one for each view. Divide each of these view groups into an equal number of smaller (about six to eight students) groups of participants who share the same viewpoint.

2. For as many sets of opposing groups as were formed, place two chairs facing another two chairs. Invite two members each from opposing groups to occupy them as the first speakers. Ask the rest of their teams to stand behind them, ready to participate.

2. Explain that one person will begin by stating their case and, when they have finished (or pause long enough), a student from the opposing side can present his or her view. Students should take turns alternately.

3. Tell students that team members may be replaced after they have spoken. The one who wishes to step in should tap the one who has spoken on the shoulder.

4. Warn teams that any interruption to a speaker from the opposing team results in the team's loss.

5. Encourage team members to replace speakers frequently, even if the new speaker simply restates a point already made.

**Metacognitive Discussion**

1. As a result of this experience, can you list the techniques of debate?

2. Did you recognize any speaker using the argument writing framework to structure what they said?

**Closure**

Ask students if any have changed their point of view as a result of participating in the piranha pool.

# Visual Language Activities

**Focus Activity** ## Political Cartoon

**Political cartoon** gives students the chance to examine and analyze political (editorial) cartoons with attention to the way they achieve their point.

## Objective

This activity helps students interpret the visual language of political cartoons.

## Input

The teacher obtains political cartoons, both old and contemporary, from newspapers. Students might be asked to bring in a favorite cartoon about a particular issue.

## Procedure

1. Show a cartoon to the class.

2. Lead students to discuss how cartoon artists achieve their aims of ridicule and comment.

## Metacognitive Discussion

What can be achieved using argument in the form of visual text that cannot be readily achieved using written text?

## Closure

Encourage students to suggest new captions for the political cartoons.

# Written Language Activities

**Focus Activity**

# Argument and Discussion Reconstruction

**Argument and discussion reconstruction** gives students the opportunity to physically manipulate chunks of argument and discussion text.

## Objective

This activity is designed to help students further develop their understanding of the structure and content of arguments and discussions.

## Input

The teacher selects and photocopies a clearly and logically organized argument or discussion. The text is cut up into arguments, counterarguments, consensus statements, background statements, and the thesis statement.

## Procedure

1. Arrange students in groups of three or four.
2. Give each group a set of the cut-up text.
3. Challenge each group to reconstruct the text, identifying the clues in the text that influenced their choice of reorganization.
4. Prompt groups to share their reconstruction with another group, discussing the reasons for differences or similarities in the reconstructed texts.

## Metacognitive Discussion

Students should be prompted to think critically about the original text in the light of their own reconstructions.

## Closure

As an extension to the above activity, appropriate for Grade 3 and above, lead students to reconstruct the text by attaching it to large sheets of paper, leaving spaces between each point or section. Then, challenge students to write additional arguments in the allotted spaces.

**Focus Activity**

# Walking in Another's Shoes

**Walking in another's shoes** is an activity in which students are asked to think from various points of view.

## Objective

This activity assists students to understand and appreciate other people's points of view, and in so doing, use this information to construct arguments and discussions.

## Input

Although this is a fun activity, students should be led to appreciate the serious side of things, that understanding where their opponent is coming from will assist them to argue or discuss with them. For example, the way a person recalls a ballgame depends, in part, on whom he or she backed to win.

## Procedure

1. Ask students to think about a topic, such as rain.

2. Encourage students to imagine how they might view rain if they were, a ditch, a cloud, a pair of boots or sneakers, a carwash attendant, a flower, a swan, a construction worker, and so forth.

3. Tell students to choose a point of view and write an argument or discussion based on the chosen view. For example, they might write about the flower's argument that rain is awesome.

## Metacognitive Discussion

Students can reflect on the power of understanding what it is like to walk in another's shoes.

## Closure

Ask students to exchange their papers. After they read and appreciate another person's point of view, request that students briefly talk to each other in a way that sympathetically reflects those views. Then challenge them to try to convince the other person that their view is the more valid one.

**Focus Activity**    # Rewrite for Today

**Rewrite for today** is an activity in which students take a famous persuasive speech and rewrite it in today's language and from the cultural perspectives of today's world.

## Objective

This activity assists student to appreciate the way persuasive language works and changes.

## Input

The teacher chooses a famous historical speech or speech extract and either prepares to read it aloud or finds a recording of the speech. Students need to receive a typed transcript of the speech, double- or even triple-spaced.

## Procedure

1. Give each student a copy of the speech, typed in double- or triple-space.

2. Read or play the speech. Ask students to discuss some of the persuasive conventions used (such as grouping points into sets of three, repeating sentence starters) and the type of language (historical or sociocultural) used.

3. Assign students in groups of two or three, to rewrite the speech, writing between the lines, in current language, and from the perspective of their world.

## Metacognitive Discussion

1. How did the language change the meaning?
2. Give reasons for your changes to the text.

## Closure

Encourage students to share their new texts. Invite them to audiotape or videotape their altered versions of the speech.

# WRITING Arguments and Discussions

CHAPTER 18

## Introduction to the Argument and Discussion Writing Model Program

The focus activities in this chapter are planned around a model program for introducing argument and discussion writing and show how activities might be brought together in a program that can last several days.

Briefly, the model program for writing arguments and discussions is a unit about a school issue, focusing on a debate about the issue of school uniforms appropriate for the middle or high school level. The types of thinking that are stressed are analyzing, which includes composing bias, composing assumptions, predicting, linking, drawing conclusions, combining ideas, ordering, and considering multiple perspectives; and evaluating, which encompasses composing analogies, making decisions, solving problems, summarizing, questioning, and predicting counterarguments. The program introduces students to the Socratic questions, discussion web, and creative problem-solving frames. The context of study for the program is a language and literacy unit.

Achievement objectives for the program are aimed to assist students in acquiring both thinking and language skills.

The oral language objectives are to help students

1. talk persuasively to small groups about their views;

2. organize their arguments and discussions so that only the most persuasive arguments are voiced;

3. listen to speakers and identify how their arguments and discussions are structured;

4. listen to speakers and counter their arguments.

The exploring language objectives are to help students

1. explore the language choices made by the authors of arguments and discussions;

2. identify the common language features of arguments and discussions, including the use of counterarguments;

3. use argument and discussion writing frames to jointly and independently construct arguments and discussions.

The arguments and discussion thinking objectives are to help students

1. use the Socratic questions frame to prepare for composing arguments and discussions;

2. use discussion web frames and the creative problem-solving frame to prepare written arguments and discussions.

To prepare for this unit, teachers need to

1. collect information from other schools regarding school uniform policy;

2. poll students on the question of whether they are for or against school uniforms;

3. obtain videos of political debates for students to view throughout the unit;

4. obtain political cartoons (from newspaper) or public health posters that argue a point of view;

5. borrow a video camera, and assign a teacher's aide to film a record of oral arguments and discussions conducted in class;

6. contact another teacher and organize a debate on the topic between teams from each class;

7. photocopy argument and discussion models on transparencies,

8. photocopy argument and discussion writing frames;

9. photocopy the Socratic questions, discussion web, and creative problem-solving thinking frames.

In this chapter, focus activities are linked to show a logical progression in the program. Session numbers are added as a reminder that an activity might use products or learning from an earlier activity.

SkyLight Training and Publishing Inc.

# Building Knowledge of the Topic

**Focus Activity**

# Interview

In the **interview**, students arrange to interview some of their peers about the topic of whether or not they should wear school uniforms. (Session 1)

**Objective**

Students build an understanding of views held by the class before writing and use these to counter other arguments.

**Input**

This activity may first require the joint construction of interview questions and some role-modeling by the whole class.

**Procedure**

1. Ask students to interview peers individually.

2. Prompt students to meet in small groups (three or four members) to pool the reasons for and against the wearing of school uniforms.

3. Instruct group members to prioritize their reasons for an issue (pros) from strongest to weakest and then prioritize the reasons against the issue (cons).

4. Ask students to design counterarguments.

5. Lead groups to share their arguments using the envoy strategy.

**Metacognitive Discussion**

Students should reflect on what makes a strong argument, how to select the weakest opposing argument, and how to effectively counter it.

**Closure**

Discuss and record students' ideas about what makes a strong argument and counterargument.

**Focus Activity** # Clarify-Pair-Share

In the **clarify-pair-share** activity, students discuss the topic with classmates. (Session 2)

**Objective**

This activity involves students in practicing how to actively listen and in using words that signal the structure of an argument.

**Input**

Students need to have conducted some research on the topic.

**Procedure**

1. Group students into pairs. Tell student 1 to select an argument (pro or con) regarding the wearing of school uniforms and state that argument to his or her partner, student 2.

2. Prompt student 1 to clarify and elaborate on the initial statement.

3. Tell student 2 to reflect back to the partner what he or she said (active listening).

4. Allow student 2 to then either counter that argument or state an opposing argument, then clarify and elaborate on it.

5. Continue this sequence until all arguments and counter-arguments have been presented.

6. Ask pairs to share their discussion with another pair or with the class.

7. Facilitate class sharing by using the signal language of arguments and discussions between speakers, such as For these reasons I believe that . . ., Another reason I believe that . . ., Finally I think that. . . .

**Metacognitive Discussion**

Students reflect on the shared presentations, identifying in particular the content and structure of the exchange.

**Closure**

Ask class members to vote to select one exchange to be shared with another class.

SkyLight Training and Publishing Inc.

**Focus Activity**   # Debate

In the **debate** activity, student pairs engage in debate with the goal of convincing the other participant of their point of view. (Session 3)

### Objective

This activity allows the teacher to assess each student's argument skills against the established criteria and format for the debate.

### Input

Students locate members of the class that hold opposite views on the topic of school uniforms. Debating teams of three students are formed and students are briefed on the agreed-upon format for debates.

### Procedure

1. Lead students, in groups of three, to design an opening argument, likely counterarguments (for the purpose of rebuttal), and a summary statement.

2. Invite groups to present their debate to the rest of the class. Encourage the class to select the winning team through acclamation.

### Metacognitive Discussion

The class audience members complete a debating skills checklist as the arguments are presented and use this to decide on the winning team.

### Closure

Ask the audience to select the winning team.

# Modeling Arguments and Discussions

 **Focus Activity**

# Model Arguments and Discussions

In this activity, teachers **model arguments and discussions** using examples and text frames and explain the structure, tense, and use of argument and discussion signal words. (Session 4)

## Objective

By the end of this activity, students should be able to list the conventions and qualities of an argument or discussion and how these are reflected in writing frames.

## Input

The teacher finds a number of model oral and written arguments and discussions that contain good examples of argument and discussion structure, tense, and appropriate signal words. Teachers have available large copies (poster-size) of the writing frames to use during the demonstrations.

## Procedure

1. Read aloud several arguments and discussions during the course of the unit.

2. Show a model text on a transparency and identify the conventions of argument and discussion. Model the use of the argument and discussion writing frames and lead the class to jointly construct part of a text.

3. Model the use of signal words and phrases by guiding the class to jointly construct words and phrases to go with argument statements debated by pairs of students.

## Metacognitive Discussion

Students might be challenged to decide whether other text types or literary genre (e.g., a poem) would allow them to or help them to argue and discuss.

## Closure

Change key words that describe arguments and discussions.

# Working With Argument and Discussion Thinking Frames

**Focus Activity** | # Modeling the Socratic Questions Frame

**Modeling the Socratic questions frame** introduces students to this thinking frame. (Session 5)

---

### Objective

By the completion of this activity students should be able to use the Socratic questions to improve the quality of their arguments and discussions.

---

### Input

The teacher needs a large copy of the Socratic questions frame to use during the discussion.

---

### Procedure

1. Explain how to use the Socratic questions frame.

2. Demonstrate the technique after reading a simple folk tale. For example, read the tale of Little Red Riding Hood and demonstrate how to use the frame to think about the statement All wolves are bad.

3. Ask students, working in small groups, to select one of their key arguments in regard to school uniforms from a previous activity. Tell students to record the statement, (such as School uniforms are uncomfortable) and apply the Socratic questions frame. For example, students might gather evidence that some students find uniforms comfortable.

4. Lead groups to record the outcomes of their discussion and select a reporter to share their results with the class.

---

### Metacognitive Discussion

Students should share any new argument points (in addition to those developed in previous activities) that emerged through the use of the Socratic questions, reflecting on how the questions assisted in generating new points.

---

### Closure

Encourage groups to share their statement and one new point that emerged from using the Socratic questions frame.

**Focus Activity** # Using the Discussion Web

**Using the discussion web** is an activity that allows students to practice this type of thinking frame. (Session 6)

## Objective

Students should demonstrate their competence with discussion webs as an outcome of this activity.

## Input

Students need to be familiar with discussion web frames. A copy should be on display for student reference during this activity. The discussion web might be used as part of a larger unit of work so that students have sufficient background knowledge and see the web as relevant.

## Procedure

1. Divide students into groups of four to six.

2. Prompt each student to record a key argument (pro or con) on the discussion web.

3. Ask each group to write a joint conclusion. (Note: This may require the group first to reach some kind of consensus about the proposition of school uniforms.)

## Metacognitive Discussion

Students should reflect on their proficiency with the discussion web and decide on what occasions the web would be useful and when it would be less appropriate.

## Closure

Invite students to share their webs with the rest of the class.

**Focus Activity** # Using the Creative Problem-Solving Frame

**Using the creative problem-solving frame** provides students with an opportunity to practice this type of thinking. (Session 7)

## Objective

Students should demonstrate their competence with the creative problem-solving frame as an outcome of this activity.

## Input

Students need to be familiar with the creative problem-solving frame. A copy should be available for viewing during the activity. The creative problem-solving frame might be used as part of a larger unit of work so that students have sufficient background knowledge and see the relevancy of the frame.

## Procedure

1. Divide students into groups of four to six.

2. Ask each group to select one problem associated with the school uniform topic. For example, one group might say, "If we don't have uniforms, some people from poorer families are going to stand out as badly dressed. This will be embarrassing for them."

3. Direct groups to use the creative problem-solving frame to resolve this problem.

## Metacognitive Discussion

Students should reflect on their proficiency with the creative problem-solving frame and decide on what occasions the frame would be useful or appropriate.

## Closure

Encourage groups to report their best solution to the class.

**Focus Activity** # Using the Perspective Frame

**Using the perspective frame** is a way to introduce students to seeing a problem from different perspectives. (Session 8)

## Objective

Students should demonstrate their competence with the perspective frame as an outcome of this activity.

## Input

A copy of the perspective frame should be available for reference during the activity. Students need to be familiar with what each perspective cue word means and to be reminded to select those words that best suit their purpose. The perspective frame might be used as part of a larger unit of work, so that students have sufficient background knowledge of the topic and see the frame as relevant.

## Procedure

1. Instruct students, working in pairs, to select one argument, pro or con, regarding the wearing of school uniforms.

2. Encourage pairs to select one or more perspectives and think about their argument from that or those perspectives. (Note: The talk perspective is a good one to begin with. The number of perspectives chosen depends on the experience of the students.)

## Metacognitive Discussion

Students should reflect on their proficiency with the perspective frame, and decide on what occasions the frame would be useful and less appropriate.

## Closure

Encourage pairs to share with the class or another group their new insights in relation to the argument.

# Working With Argument and Discussion Writing Frames

**Focus Activity**

# Writing Together

**Writing together** is an activity in which students prepare an argument or discussion in small groups using the writing frame for arguments or discussions. (Session 9)

---

**Objective**

Students should demonstrate their competence in the use of the writing frame.

---

**Input**

Students need to be familiar with the writing frame for either argument or discussion, depending on which they choose to produce. It would be helpful if the class could brainstorm a list of possible arguments before students break into groups. Depending on the students' background knowledge, this brainstorming process may not take long.

---

**Procedure**

1. Lead the class as a whole to choose whether to write an argument or a discussion. Or, alternatively, allow individual groups decide for themselves which form to write.

2. Divide students into groups of three or four.

3. Ask each group member to select one argument to work on.

4. After each group member has developed an argument in note form, encourage the groups to use the argument writing frame to jointly draft a text.

5. Instruct groups to prepare one jointly constructed text for publication.

---

**Metacognitive Discussion**

Students should discuss whether they still need to use a writing frame for drafting their written texts.

---

**Closure**

Lead students to discuss how the jointly constructed arguments or discussions might be revised for different audiences and how/if the text achieved its purposes.

**Focus Activity**

# Writing Independently

**Writing independently** gives students the opportunity to produce an argument or discussion on their own. (Session 10)

## Objective

Students should demonstrate their competence in writing explanations.

## Input

Teachers should alert students the previous day that they will write an argument or discussion on an issue of their choice, that they may need to do some research, and that they will need to select a thinking frame to assist them in developing their topic. Indicate to students that this activity will provide a measure of how well they can apply the knowledge and skills introduced during the course of the study.

## Procedure

1. Prompt students to decide on their purpose for writing and their audience before they begin writing.

2. Encourage students to select a thinking strategy and to then draft and later publish an argument or discussion. You might choose to have some less independent students draft their text on a writing frame and confer with you, but most students should compose their texts independently.

3. Challenge students to share their published texts with their peers and to respond to their audience.

4. Lead students to assess their own arguments and discussions using both comment from their peers and the following criteria:

   • Was the meaning clear?

   • Was it well-structured?

   • How well did I do with the spelling and punctuation?

   • How confident am I about writing arguments and discussions?

5. Ask students who used a thinking frame to also assess what effect it had on their writing. (Possible frames include the Socratic questions, the discussion web, the creative problem-solving, and the perspective frames.)

6. Use the argument and discussion writing assessment rubric to record students' progress with this form of thinking and writing.

## Metacognitive Discussion

Students discuss the effect of the argument and discussion writing frames on their writing and whether they would like to continue using them.

## Closure

Lead students to discuss whether they can identify the characteristics of arguments and discussions, whether they enjoyed the experience, and whether they have new writing goals.

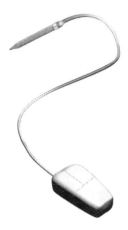

# Bibliography

Applebee, A. N. 1978. *The child's concept of story: Ages two to seventeen*. Chicago: University of Chicago Press.

Baynton, M. 1988. *Jane and the dragon*. Auckland, New Zealand: Scholastic.

Belting, Natalia. 1965. *The Earth is on a fish's back: Tales of beginnings*. New York: Henry Holt and Company.

Bereiter, C. and M. Scardamalia. 1982. From conversation to composition: The role of instruction in a developmenal process. In *Advances in instructional psychology*, edited by R. Glaser. Hillsdale, N. J.: Lawrence Erlbaum.

Bruner, J. 1986. *Actual mind, possible worlds*. Cambridge, Mass.: Harvard University Press.

Cairney, T. 1990. Intertextuality: Infectious echoes of the past. *Reading Teacher* 43(7): 478–484.

Callaghan, M., P. Knapp, and G. Noble. 1993. Genre in practice. In *The powers of literacy: A genre approach to teaching writing*, edited by B. Cope and M. Kalantis. London: Falmer Press.

Cudd, E., and L. Roberts. 1989. Using writing to enhance content area learning in the primary grades. *Reading Teacher* 42(6): 392–404.

Donaldson, M. 1978. *Children's minds*. London: Fontana.

Eberle, B. 1996. *SCAMPER: Creative games and activities for imagination development*. Waco, Tex.: Prufrock Press.

Eggins, S., J. R. Martin, and P. Wignell. 1987. The discourse of geography. *Working Papers in Linguisitics* (University of Sydney Linguistics Department) 5: 54–56.

Flower, L., and J. Hayes. 1984. Images, plans, and prose: The representation of meaning in writing. *Written Communication* 1(1): 120–160.

Fogarty, R., and J. Bellanca. 1986. *Teach them thinking: Mental menus for 24 thinking skills*. Palatine, Ill.: IRI/SkyLight Training and Publishing Inc.

———. 1991. *Blueprints for thinking in the cooperative classroom*. 2d ed. Palatine, Ill.: IRI/SkyLight Training and Publishing Inc.

Graves, D. 1983. *Writing: Teachers and children at work.* Exeter, N.H.: Heinemann Education Books.

Hewings, M., and M. J. McCarthy. 1988. An alternative approach to the analysis of text. *Praxis des Neusprachlichen Unterrichts* 1: 3–10.

Jukes, M. 1984. *Like Jake and me.* New York: Dragonfly Books.

Lipman, M. 1991. *Thinking in education.* Cambridge, England: Cambridge University Press.

Martin, J. R. 1985. *Factual writing: Exploring and challenging social reality.* Oxford, England: Oxford University Press.

McCarthy, B., and S. Carter. 1994. Response to Western culture in EFL language instruction, by J. D. Heiman. *TESOL Journal* 3(4): 7–16.

Paul, R. W. 1991. Dialogical and dialectical thinking. *In Developing minds: A resource book for teaching thinking,* edited by A. L. Costa. Alexandria, Va.: Association for Supervision and Curriculum Development.

Reppens, R. 1994. A genre-based approach to content area writing instruction. *TESOL Journal* 4: 32–35.

Rothery, J. 1986. *Teaching writing in the primary school: A genre based approach to the development of writing abilities.* Sydney, Australia: University of Sydney, Department of Linguistics.

Vygostsky, L. S. 1978. *Mind in society.* Cambridge, Mass.: Harvard University Press.

Wagner, J. 1989. *Aranea.* New York: Puffin.

Wray, D., and M. Lewis. 1995. *Developing children's non-fiction writing: Working with writing frames.* London: Scholastic.

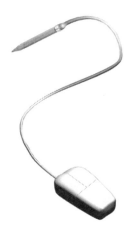

# Index

SkyLight Training and Publishing Inc.

SkyLight Training and Publishing Inc.

SkyLight Training and Publishing Inc.

# We Prepare Your Teachers Today for the Classrooms of Tomorrow

*Learn from Our Books and from Our Authors!*

## Ignite Learning in Your School or District.

SkyLight's team of classroom-experienced consultants can help you foster systemic change for increased student achievement.

**Professional development is a process, not an event.** SkyLight's seasoned practitioners drive the creation of our on-site professional development programs, graduate courses, research-based publications, interactive video courses, teacher-friendly training materials, and online resources—call SkyLight Training and Publishing Inc. today.

**SkyLight specializes in three professional development areas.**

Specialty # **1**

### Best Practices

We **model** the best practices that result in improved student performance and guided applications.

Specialty # **2**

### Making the Innovations Last

We help set up **support** systems that make innovations part of everyday practice in the long-term systemic improvement of your school or district.

Specialty # **3**

### How to Assess the Results

We prepare your school leaders to encourage and **assess** teacher growth, **measure** student achievement, and **evaluate** program success.

*Contact the SkyLight team and begin a process toward long-term results.*

2626 S. Clearbrook Dr., Arlington Heights, IL 60005
800-348-4474 • 847-290-6600 • FAX 847-290-6609
http://www.iriskylight.com

There are

one-story intellects,

two-story intellects, and three-story

intellects with skylights. All fact collectors, who

have no aim beyond their facts, are one-story men. Two-story men

compare, reason, generalize, using the labors of the fact collectors as

well as their own. Three-story men idealize, imagine,

predict—their best illumination comes from

above, through the skylight.

—*Oliver Wendell*

*Holmes*

SkyLight

Training and Publishing Inc.